HARD TIMES
Easy Trading

A Simple Guide to Generating Consistent Income in any Economy

JIM PETERSON

Hard Times Easy Trading: A Simple Guide to Generating Consistent Income in any Economy
Published by Income Strategies Academy, LLC
305 Tequesta Dr
Destin, Florida 32541

For more information, please e-mail us:
info@incomestrategiesacademy.com
or visit our website at: www.incomestrategiesacademy.com

All rights reserved. No part of this book may be reproduced in any form or by any electronic or mechanical means including information storage and retrieval systems without permission in writing from the copyright holder, except by a reviewer, who may quote brief passages in review.

ISBN-13: 978-0615488189
ISBN-10: 0615488188

Copyright© 2011 by Jim Peterson

The examples of specific companies that are used in this book are only for educational purposes and are not recommendations. The author is not licensed or engaged in providing legal, accounting, securities sales, or other professional services. Stock and options trading has large potential rewards but also large potential risk. You must be aware of these risks, and be willing to accept them, in order to invest in the stock, derivatives, or option markets. The author assumes no liability for damages either directly or indirectly arising from the use or misuse of this book.

Every investor who uses options should read and understand the publication *Characteristics and Risks of Standardized Options*. A copy can be obtained free of charge from The Chicago Board Options Exchange (1-800-OPTIONS) or from your broker. The investor considering options should consult their tax advisor as to how taxes may affect the outcome of contemplated options transactions. A prospectus, which discusses the role of the Options Clearing Corporation, is also available without charge upon request at the Options Clearing Corporation, 440 S LaSalle St, Suite 908, Chicago, Illinois 60605.

TABLE OF CONTENTS

FOREWORD xi
PREFACE xiii
ACKNOWLEDGMENTS. xvii
INTRODUCTION xix
CHAPTER 1: ENHANCE YOUR LIFE AND SECURE YOUR RETIREMENT. 1

   Generate a monthly income by selling
option premium 1

   Types of Investing. 4

   The hazards of using a long-term buy-and-hold
investment strategy 4

   Day-trading is a full time job 6

   Income trading can create less risk and stable returns . . 7

   Determine the exact odds of placing a winning trade . . 9

   The winning recipe 10

CHAPTER 2: MASTER THE PSYCHOLOGY OF INVESTING.... 13
    How Little George achieved financial success..... 13
    Embrace the mind-set that you will never fail..... 14
    Just like the "house" in a casino, put the odds of winning in your favor.................. 15
    Your investment or retirement account is serious business..................... 16
    Trading rules 17
    Define your investment goals 18

CHAPTER 3: THE MIRACLE OF COMPOUND INTEREST 21
    Let compound interest work in your favor 23
    Set your income goal at 3–5 percentper month.... 24
    Always write down the rules of the trade 26
    The Rule of 72 27

CHAPTER 4: ACHIEVE YOUR DREAMS 29
    You can achieve your dreams 29
    Goal-setting is necessary 30
    Maintain a positive attitude.............. 33
    Have a trading plan.................. 33
    Keeping good records—the best sign of success.... 34

CHAPTER 5: SAVE MONEY THROUGH SMART ACCOUNT OPENING 35
    Different types of accounts 35

Lower your commissions 37
Avoid "trade for a hobby" brokerage firms 37

CHAPTER 6: MAKE EASY MONEY BY UNDERSTANDING INDEXES AND ETFS 39

Avoid mutual funds................... 40
Index investing—low commissions and broad diversification...................... 40
The advantages of investing in ETFs 42

CHAPTER 7: SELECTING AND TIMING YOUR STOCK PURCHASES.......................... 45

Defining price 45
Technical analysis—one of the keys to success 47
Why technical analysis works.............. 48
Trend following your way to profits........... 49
Charting—a way to "forecast" future price movements 50
The rules of trend following: 51
Support and resistance 52
Put the odds in your favor 54
Technical indicators................... 54
Moving averages 55
MACD: The strongest indicator of future price movement...................... 57
Stochastic—the timing indicator 60

The Elder-Ray Indicator 62
Channeling bands 64

CHAPTER 8: PUT THE ODDS IN YOUR FAVOR—USE OPTIONS . 67

Options defined 67
Limit risk and increase return on investment 68
Call options. 69
Put options 70
Use options to insure your portfolio 72
Options terminology 75
Options pricing. 77
Option Profits—step-by-step rules 79

CHAPTER 9: DECREASING YOUR RISK 81

The covered call strategy 84
Lower your risk and increase your income 85
Assessing the risks. 86
You can shift the risk and put the odds in your favor . 87

CHAPTER 10: INSTANT INCOME THROUGH SELLING COVERED CALLS 89

Rules of the stock selection process 89
Sources for screening stocks. 90
Use technical analysis to time purchases and sells . . . 92
A covered call example 94
Technical indicators. 95

CHAPTER 11: LEAPS: ACHIEVE HUGE PROFITS BY EMPLOYING FINANCIAL LEVERAGE 105

    Be Like Lance! 105

    Financial leverage 107

    LEAPS defined 108

    LEAPS—the risk factors 110

    Success with LEAPS—the reasons 111

    Use LEAPS to increase your buying power 112

    Steps to using LEAPS as a stock substitute: 114

    How to calculate yield comparisons when
using LEAPS 116

CHAPTER 12: THE SECRET OF SYNTHETIC STOCK POSITIONS . 127

    The synthetic stock position 127

    The synthetic covered call 128

CHAPTER 13: PROTECT YOUR PROFITS THROUGH HEDGING . 131

    Buy protective puts correctly 131

    Insure Your Portfolio with Protective Puts 133

CONCLUSION 137

APPENDIX 1: A LOOK AT DIRECTIONAL TRADING 141

APPENDIX 2: HOW TO "SHOOT FOR THE STARS" WITHOUT LOSING YOUR SHIRT 145

APPENDIX 3: GLOSSARY 149

APPENDIX 4: EXHIBITS 162

FOREWORD

I met Jim Peterson several years ago, when he attended one of the "Power to Prosper" seminars that I lead several times each year. Over the time that we have known each other, I have become aware of his vast knowledge and experience across the entire investment spectrum. For many decades, Jim has been involved in making major investment decisions for both large financial institutions and individual investors.

Jim began his professional career by serving for eight years as an investment analyst and portfolio manager at a major money management institution. There he did primary research, made recommendations, and advised the portfolio managers on their stock equity holdings.

He was a founder and general partner of Peterson Properties of Atlanta, Georgia, which developed, leased, and managed in excess of four million square feet of commercial buildings. Peterson Properties was sold to an NYSE listed company in 1996 for in excess of $146 million.

Jim served as a managing director of CarrAmerica ("CRE"), an NYSE-listed real estate investment trust. There he was responsible for its Florida operations, including the purchase of in excess of $300 million in investment properties. CRE was sold to The Blackstone Group for $5.6 billion in 2006.

Jim also served as a director, CEO, and chief investment officer (CIO) of Investment Life of America ("ILA"), where he was the managing director of an investment income portfolio with a value of in excess of $100 million.

Jim has a Bachelor of Science degree in business administration from the University of North Carolina at Chapel Hill and an MBA from the University of Texas at Austin. He holds a real estate license and a general contractor's license in the state of Florida.

Jim has studied options trading for a number of years and has been engaged in actual trading. He is not teaching and writing from a theoretical point of view. He is an actual trader who teaches from a trader's perspective.

Reading his book and attending Jim's seminar has opened up a world to me that I did not know existed only a short time ago. It has certainly enhanced my financial future. If you take the time to study and employ the lessons of this book, I believe that it will enrich your future also.

—Larry J. Raad

PREFACE

Do you need more income in order to support your family in the lifestyle that they deserve? Has your 401(k), IRA, or other retirement plan lost so much value that you will not be able to live out your remaining years in the lifestyle that, just a short time ago, you believed you would? Are you in a position in which you cannot make your monthly mortgage, credit card, and other payments?

If you, like so many other Americans, are in one or more of these positions, then you can change your whole life and your future by reading this book and applying the techniques revealed in it. It was written in a time of worldwide financial crisis, but the strategies taught in it were applicable before the crisis started, and they will be applicable after it is finished.

You need to learn how to manage your own money! In late 2008, television and newspapers were full of news about the Bernard Madoff scandal. It has been called the largest Ponzi scheme in history. It is believed that Madoff, through his investment advisory firm, brokerage firm, and hedge fund stole as much as $50 billion of his clients' money. For many of these people, their lives will never be the same again.

The lesson to be learned from the Madoff scandal (and other money management scandals) is that it is foolish of you to allow other people to manage your money. No one cares as much about your money as you do. No one will devote the care and time necessary to increase your return or to guard your principal as you will. You owe it to yourself and your family to learn the basics of investing and to take charge of managing your money. When you manage your money, you *are* managing your life and your family's future.

Do not put yourself in a position of waking up one day only to find that you are broke and too old to get a job. Learning to manage your own money and to make it work for you is a never-ending process, and you need to start right now.

There is a small group of professional investors, traders, and market makers that achieve consistent monthly income from trading stocks and options on the CBOE (Chicago Board of Exchange) and other options exchanges. They do this by employing specific time-tested *income trading* techniques. These methods are referred to as being "non-directional," because they are designed to be profitable whether the stock market goes up, down, or sideways.

Many of the people who successfully employ these techniques make all of the money that they want or need from their trading activities. Not only do they have little or no incentive to teach their methods to other people, they are afraid that if too many people learn their techniques, these systems will no longer be successful. Therefore, it is difficult for an ordinary retail investor to find an opportunity to learn income trading.

I wrote this book in order to reveal some of their trading secrets to small retail investors. I also teach seminars that take people to the next level, if they are dedicated to achieving financial success through income trading. As a condition to being accepted into one these seminars, one must acknowledge an obligation to give back a portion of the wealth that they acquire to less fortunate people.

If you want to learn advanced techniques on how to secure your future with a trading plan that is non-directional, generates high income, and has lower risk than merely owning stocks and/or bonds, then read this book and then *attend one of the income trading seminars that you can find at www.incomestrategiesacademy.com.*

Getting an education is not something that one does for a short while and is then finished. It is a lifelong journey. Acquiring a financial education is the same. Good luck in your journey; I wish you the best!

ACKNOWLEDGMENTS

Over the course of the one and one-half years during which I devoted a great deal of time to writing this book, my wife, Mylene, became pregnant and gave birth to twins, a boy and a girl. Not only did she endure the hardship of carrying two babies in her small, 105-pound body frame, she also put up with the battle of fatigue of taking care of two newborn babies without much help from me, while I worked on this manuscript and gave speeches and seminars. I dedicate this book to her in an effort to express my gratitude to her and to my newborn children, James Paul and Jalene Helen. Without her encouragement and persuasion to complete the task, I would not have ever finished writing it.

INTRODUCTION

The year 2008 was the beginning of a financial crisis, not only in the United States, but worldwide. Real estate values fell to levels that, only one year earlier, people believed were not possible. A mortgage loan changed from something that was easy to obtain and available to everyone into something that was difficult, if not impossible, to obtain. Many people had been using their homes as their piggybanks for decades by refinancing every few years as home values increased in order to put spending money in their pockets. This cash flow provided the money to buy new cars, expensive vacations, and fancy electronic equipment.

In late 2008, we were warned that the major financial institutions would go bankrupt unless the federal government bailed them out. The unemployment rate began to skyrocket to levels not seen in decades. It was forecast that unemployment might even go to levels not seen since the 1930s. People were losing their source of income and their means of supporting their families. They were being forced out of their homes and had no place to live. As this trend continued into

2009 and 2010, giant government spending programs were authorized under the guise of bank and other corporate bailouts. Even auto and other companies were being first bailed out and then taken over by the federal government.

The stock market lost over 40 percent of its value in 2008. There was talk of Social Security defaulting on future payments and the nationalization of 401(k) and other retirement funds.

> **Option:** A security that gives the holder the right to buy (call option) or to sell (put option) a particular asset at a certain price (the strike price) on or before a certain date (the expiration date). This is a right to exercise; it is not an obligation to do so.

Yet a small group of investors continued to do just fine. They are non-directional income traders. They deal in collecting premium income from selling **options** that are covered by a hedge position on the CBOE and other financial exchanges. They do this by employing techniques that anyone can learn. This book is a beginning lesson on how any ordinary retail investor can easily start profiting by using certain of these techniques in their own investing and trading. You can use these techniques to your benefit, either as a means of making a living or as a part-time investor, in order to change your life and retirement years into a more enjoyable experience for you and your family.

The investing techniques described in this book, and other more advanced techniques that can only be learned through live seminars and one-on-one mentoring sessions, have been developed over decades by mathematicians, investors, and traders. They are methods by which experts consistently make money in the stock and options market.

When I first heard that these consistent money-making techniques existed, I was determined to learn them and how to use them to benefit myself and my family. However, there is one large problem in acquir-

> **Directional Trading:** A position or combination of positions in securities and/or options that rely upon appreciation or depreciation in the price of such security in order for the trade to be profitable.

ing this knowledge: it is difficult to find someone who is willing to teach it to others. If someone is making all of the money that he desires by trading his personal account, then he has little incentive to devote the time and effort necessary to teach others how to share these same advantages. So, while these methods are actually easy to learn, it is very difficult to find educational material on them, or the person who will teach them to you. Consequently, most investors merely continue to make **directional trades** that sometimes make money and sometimes lose money.

I hope that my time and efforts spent in compiling the material in this book will be helpful to you. If they are, and if you want to go further in achieving financial success, then I hope to see you at one of my future seminars in order that you might learn the advanced techniques that can bring monetary security to you and your family. Information on seminars and other educational materials can be found at www.incomestrategiesacademy.com.

CHAPTER 1

Enhance Your Life and Secure Your Retirement

> Money is the sixth sense that makes it
> possible to enjoy the other five.
> —**Richard Ney**

Generate a monthly income by selling option premium

The purpose of this book is to educate you on how to survive financially, not only in an economic crisis, but for the rest of your life, by using certain common **stock** and stock option income strategies that have proven to be successful when employed by professional investors and traders, market makers, hedge fund operators, and even retail traders in order to generate a stable monthly income. Will these strategies or any other

> **Stock:** Evidence of an ownership position in a company.

investment strategy work every time you use them? No! But, if used correctly and consistently, they can provide you with an opportunity to greatly enhance your financial future and your life by increasing the value of your investment and retirement funds. In fact, they can teach you how to generate a monthly income for the rest of your life.

> **Option Premium:** The price that a holder pays in order to acquire or to sell an option.

> **ETF:** Exchange Traded Fund. An investment fund that is traded on stock exchanges, much like stocks. An ETF holds assets, such as stocks or bonds, and trades at approximately the same price as the net asset value of its underlying assets over the course of the trading day. Most ETFs track either an index, such as the S&P 500, or stocks in a specific industry or sector. For this reason, the specific stocks do not change often as with an actively managed mutual fund. ETFs may be attractive as investments because of their low management fees, tax efficiency, and stock-like features.

This book describes some of the beginning processes by which an ordinary retail investor can learn to use options to generate a monthly income. It will also explain one of the more common uses of options, which is to hedge or insure a portfolio against market downturns.

I have talked to a number of market makers. Most of them do not have very much capital or even own their seats on an exchange, yet they make enough money every month to make the lease payment on their exchange seat (about $20,000 per month as of this writing) and also to support their families. How do they do this? They do it primarily by generating income through selling **option premium**. "Option premium" is the cash generated by selling your right to benefit from a large movement in a common stock, **ETF (exchange-traded fund)**, or **index**. Do you know who many people believe to be the largest buyer and seller of options in the entire world? The answer is: Warren Buffet's Berkshire Hathaway Company. Is Buffet a speculator? No. What is he? He is an informed and knowledgeable investor. In this book, I will explain how you can employ some of the same techniques that are used not only by Warren Buffet, but also by many successful hedge fund managers in order to consistently outperform the market.

> **Index:** A compilation of stocks that are averaged together in order to obtain a price reading or measurement. Broad-based indexes such as the S&P 500 (SPX), Dow Jones Industrials (DJI), Russell 2000 (RUT), and the NASDAQ 100 (NDX) are the most commonly used indexes. There are also many narrow-based indexes. The use of these instruments allows the holder to invest based on broad economic factors as opposed to company-specific events.

Let's first examine why you are reading this book.

1. Are you approaching retirement age and realize that you do not have enough money in your retirement account to live on for the rest of your life, even when supplemented by social security? Do you believe that you will actually receive any social security? Have you recognized that, if you receive anything from social security, it will be a large reduction from that which has been promised to you?

2. Have you either lost a job or suffered a reduction in income as a result of corporate downsizing or due to the current economic crisis?

3. Do you have a business that just does not generate the income it used to?

4. Do you just want to increase the return on your (perhaps diminished) 401(k), IRA, or other retirement savings?

5. Do you want to get rich? This book is not about making a quick fortune. But, if employed over time, the techniques described herein can build substantial wealth.

Types of Investing

There are many types of investing. Each investor must discover and choose the one that is best for his psychological makeup and lifestyle. Let's examine some of them:

The hazards of using a long-term buy-and-hold investment strategy

> **Bull Market:** A stock market cycle in which prices of the broad indexes rise for an extended period of time. It is usually during a time of an expanding economy and increasing corporate profits.

A **bull market** is one in which the value of the major stock market indexes rises on average over a specified period of time.

A **bear market** is one in which the value of the major stock indexes declines on average over a specified period of time. During the long-term bull market lasting from 1981 until about 2000, most people became conditioned to believe that long-term buy-and-hold was the safest and most successful investment strategy. Buy-and-hold investors generally use **fundamental analysis** to evaluate whether or not a particular industry or a specific company is an acceptable investment. If it is, they will consider purchasing its common stock and then sitting back and watching its value grow. This strategy implies that one should not try to time entries and exits, because timing attempts will only result in missing the really big moves upward. When using this strategy, you should only invest in companies that are growing. If you pay too much to get in, this is thought to be okay, because the growth will bail you out in the long run. The high-tech bubble burst in 2000–2003 mostly put an end to this type of thinking and to people being comfortable using a long-term buy-and-hold investment strategy. If this burst was not the final nail in the coffin of this strategy, then the 2008 market meltdown certainly was. After that, even the diehard fundamentalists like the "conflict of interest crowd" that regularly appear on the popular financial TV programs no longer preach "buy and hold" for the long term.

> **Bear Market:** A stock market cycle in which prices of the broad indexes fall at least 20 percent over a period lasting at least two quarters. It is usually accompanied by a weak economy and declining corporate profits.

> **Fundamental Analysis:** The process of accessing the value of a company's stock by studying its historical financial and accounting records and its forecasts for the future. This valuation assessment is then compared to the current market price of the stock in order to form a buy or sell opinion or recommendation.

Some investment gurus preach the "random walk theory." They believe that everyone has equal access to all of the information that is legally available about every public company. Therefore, except for illegal trading that is based on insider information, this common knowledge is already priced into every stock, and no one can gain an advantage over anyone else through fundamental analysis. On this basis, they recommend buy-and-hold investing only in broad indexes such as the S&P 500 Index (SPX). However, considering the fact that even this very broad index declined over 40 percent in 2008, I believe that employing the random walk strategy can be very risky. Can you afford a 40 percent decline in your money?

Because of the heavy redemption rate in mutual funds in the fourth quarter of 2008, it is a known fact that many people who have a long-term buy-and-hold philosophy actually got out at the bottom of the market in 2008, after the major indexes were down 40 percent or more. These people will most likely follow their broker's recommendations and get back into the market when it is near the next top.

Day-trading is a full time job

> **Margin Requirement:** The amount of cash that is required to be in an account in order to execute or maintain a particular transaction.

It is possible to learn how to day-trade in order to make a living. This usually involves taking large leveraged positions based on intraday technical indicators and holding them for a short period of time, usually from five minutes up to several hours. Day traders usually look to profit from a one-quarter or a one-half point move in a stock. Day traders have reduced **margin requirements** and usually need to trade in large enough quantities to enable them to negotiate a reduced commission rate. Day traders are not permitted to hold positions overnight.

Although I have known some successful day traders, it is a high-risk business that requires a person's full attention, as well as years of experience and much intestinal fortitude, in order to master it. Most people who try day-trading give up when neither their pocketbook nor their nerves can stand it any longer.

Income trading can create less risk and stable returns

Income trading is the primary emphasis of this book. Successful income traders do the following things, all of which we will cover:

- Make entry and exit decisions based on trends, technical indicators, and the **option Greeks**, which will be explained later in this book.

> **Option Greeks:** The five mathematical calculations that determine the price of an option. These are as follows: delta, theta, gamma, rho, and vega.

- Rely on charts to help in decision making.

- Have a written game plan that includes a goal or target return, adjustment points, and a maximum loss for every trade. This game plan must be defined prior to entering the trade, and cannot be changed during the trade.

- Have a defined holding period—usually thirty to sixty days or less—then reevaluate the position.
- Always have time value, or **"theta,"** working in their favor. The only thing that we know for certain is that time will pass. Your trade position should always be profitable with the passage of time, assuming that both the price and volatility of the underlying security remain unchanged. Later in this book, we will discuss how to do this using options.

> **Theta:** Theta is a measurement of the daily rate of depreciation of an option contract's price based upon the assumption that the underlying stock remains stagnant. Thus, it is referring to the loss in value that is due to the passing of time or extrinsic value depreciation.

- Monitor their positions daily. Income trading does not have to be a full-time job, especially if the trader uses **contingency orders**. It does, however, require daily monitoring.
- Income traders seek consistent performance every month—not a few home runs.

> **Contingency Order:** An order that is placed with a broker but cannot be executed until a certain event occurs. This event is usually based upon the future price movement of the security. In most circumstances, contingency orders allow the investor to rely on the fact that his stop loss will not be greatly exceeded except in the event of a large price gap.

Determine the exact odds of placing a winning trade

In order to be successful in your investing, you must learn how to put the odds in your favor, just as if you were allowed to go around to the back of the tables at a casino and make the same bets that the house is making!

The markets have periods of volatility and periods of relative calm. Every stock or index has its own historical volatility that is measured by the standard deviation of its annual price movement. The expected volatility of the *future* price movement is called **"implied volatility,"** and it, together with the price of the underlying security, determines the price or value of any given option. You can decide that you want to deal in options that have a high percentage chance of winning and therefore a lower return; or you can decide that you want the higher returns associated with a lower probability of success. As you learn income trading techniques, you will become familiar with how to determine the exact odds of making a profit in any particular time frame or on any specific trade.

> **Implied Volatility:** The expected future (as opposed to historical) rate of change in the price of a financial asset; implied volatility is a major factor in determining the price of options.

If you can learn to successfully income trade, then you can substitute the money earned from it for your monthly income from working forty hours, or more, every week. This is done by creating investment income from selling the time value portion of option premium. I do not know whether the stock market will go up or down tomorrow, next week, next month, or next year. But I do know that tomorrow, next week, next month, and next year will come! There is value and therefore money to be made with the passing of time.

> **Non-directional Trade:** A position or combination of positions in stocks and/or options that is designed to be profitable if the underlying security trades within a narrow range rather than appreciating or depreciating by a large amount.

In order to be a successful income trader, you cannot spend time and risk money trying to be a day trader or a speculator. You must not buy on "hot tips" from an acquaintance or a friendly broker. You must forget the idea that you can be successful using a buy-and-hold strategy. Rather, you should dedicate your investment education to the techniques of **non-directional income trading**. Study, learn, and practice, and you can learn how to make money while you are sleeping or resting on a beach!

The winning recipe

In conclusion to this introduction about the type of investor that you wish to become, I remember a recent potluck dinner that my wife and I attended at our church. There were many delicious and elaborately prepared dishes there. My wife, who is a good cook herself, commented on one, "I sure wish that I could have the recipe for that dish." Why did she say that? Because she knew that if she had that step-by-step recipe, then she could prepare that dish, and it would taste just as good as the one that we were eating there at church.

There is a lesson to be learned from that episode. If you will study and practice the things that are taught in this book and in the seminars and mentoring sessions that are available to you at www.incomestrategiesacademy.com, then you will have the recipe that you need to achieve your greatest financial dreams. Do not pass up opportunity when it stares you in the face.

CHAPTER 2

Master the Psychology of Investing

> Why not go out on a limb?
> That's where the fruit is.
> —**Mark Twain**

How Little George achieved financial success

During the 1970s, I was the senior vice president responsible for the real estate investment department at a large financial institution. During this time, I met a man who was called by his friends and business acquaintances simply "Little George." I remember once when he was trying to figure out how to come up with the money that he needed in order to make a large investment in a new commercial real estate development. He talked about selling another project, but that would take too long. He talked about bringing in partners that would put up money in return for a share of the profits. He discussed various possible terms of borrowing from banks by securing the loan with other properties that he owned. Then he said good-day, and went to the hotel where he was staying.

The next morning, I met him for breakfast to discuss whether or not he thought he would spend any more time and money attempting to go forward with the transaction that we were negotiating. The first thing that he said was, "Okay, I've got the money. Let's go forward with the deal."

I replied, "But how did you do that so fast, overnight, when no one was even available to talk to you?" He replied, "Oh, I don't mean that I have it with me right now. I mean that, while I was sleeping, it came to me as to how to come up with the cash that I need to get the entire deal done. I'll have the money by the end of the week."

The point of this story is that Little George was a man of vision and faith. He knew what he wanted to do, and he believed that he could get it done. Once he had a plan, nothing could stop him from carrying it out. He believed that he *could* do it, so he just did it. In your life and in your investment planning, you need to be as positive and as confident as Little George.

Embrace the mind-set that you will never fail

You must determine within your mind that you will never fail. Do not let anyone ever discourage you or get in the way of your goals. Provided your goals are within the laws of man and God, if you believe that you can be successful in accomplishing them, then there is nothing and no one that can stop you.

Unfortunately, most people are doomed to fail in achieving their investment goals. This is because all of their lives they have been conditioned to fail.

Just like the "house" in a casino, put the odds of winning in your favor

Most people will never win at the game of stock market investing simply because they will not enter the game with the winning attitude. The stock market is the biggest casino in the world. Most people play to lose, just as they go into a casino to lose. Of course, they do not consciously believe or recognize that they want to lose, but they approach investing as a hobby or a game. I have been into many casinos with friends who said to me before entering, "Well, I have only $1,000 to lose. Once that's gone, I'll stop for the night." I have rarely been with someone who said, "If I *win* $1,000, then, based on the dollar amount of my average bet, I will know that the tables are about to turn, and I'll stop playing and keep my winnings until next time."

Did you see the movie *Ocean's Thirteen*? The "good guys" not only had to rig the tables so that the crowd would win $500 million from the casino, but they also had to simulate an earthquake in order to close the casino. They knew that gamblers have no control over themselves, and that they will always lose their winnings back to the casino if given the opportunity. They actually had to simulate an earthquake to get the people all the way out of the casino in order to protect them from their own instincts and thereby force them to keep their winnings! Do not allow yourself to become intoxicated with the action of the markets. Take your profits and your exit when the time is appropriate.

Your investment or retirement account is serious business

You can succeed at stock market trading only if you approach it as a serious business pursuit. Prior to entering a trade, you should calculate the odds of winning and then follow your plan. If you allow your emotions to enter into your decision-making process, then you are in trouble. Always practice sound money management techniques. This means to always limit your losses by risking only calculated amounts of capital.

> **Commission:** A fee that is charged by the brokerage firm that handles a transaction.

> **Slippage:** The amount of money that is lost on each trade that is attributable to the fact that one must buy at or near the asked price and sell at or near the offered price.

> Everyone in the stock market is out for themselves, as opposed to the business world, where producers, suppliers, and customers usually better themselves by helping out others.

The stock market is the most difficult game in the world. People can learn to place bets in a casino such that the odds are very close to fifty-fifty. But the stock market is a less-than-zero-sum game. Why? Because of **commissions** and **slippage**. Slippage is the amount of money lost on each trade that is attributable to the fact that one must buy at or near the asked price, and sell at or near the offered price. Everyone in the stock market is out for themselves, as opposed to the business world, where producers, suppliers, and customers usually better themselves by helping out others.

While most people spend their time looking to initiate trades, it is most often actually what you do *after* the trade is placed that determines whether you are a winner or a loser. If you are trading an amount of money that is significant to you or that determines your family income for this month, then it is not possible to avoid your emotions getting in the way of rational decision making. Therefore, you will only win the game by creating rules of trading that you set out *in writing* before you ever enter the trade. You must then follow your own rules until you exit the position. *Never change the rules during the trade.* If you need to change your rules, then do so before entering the next trade and then stick to them while that trade remains active.

Later in this book, we will discuss rules for income trading. However, you should always follow the rules below.

Trading rules

- Trade only in liquid markets. This means to deal in securities and indexes wherein the daily volume is great enough that you will not get caught in an illiquid market or one in which you cannot quickly exit your position except at a highly discounted price.

- Use **limit orders**. A limit order is one which is placed with a maximum purchase price or a minimum sale price. Do not submit an order to "buy at the market price."

> **Limit Order:** An order that is placed with a maximum price to be paid in the case of a buy, or long position, or a minimum price with respect to a sell, or short position.

- Buy or sell only at **stop loss** points or **target** points. We will discuss stops and targets later. For now, it is only necessary to know that a target price is the one at which you have reached your profit goal, and a stop price is the one at which you have reached the maximum that you are willing to lose on a trade.

> **Stop Loss:** A price or other point, such as a certain dollar amount of loss at which a position will be exited and the losses will therefore be stopped.

> **Target:** Either the price or a specific dollar profit level at which a position will be exited. It is generally the goal or desired outcome of a trade.

- Always keep accurate records of *all* your transactions, including notes on why you bought or sold and what you would do differently next time.
- Never rush a trade. Take your time to get the position and price that you want.
- Never get greedy, when you reach your predetermined desired profit target, sell and take it.
- Never change the trade rules while you are in a trade. As you gain knowledge and experience, if you want to change your trade rules, do so before you enter the next trade and then follow your new rules until that trade is finished.

Define your investment goals

1. The first goal of your personal investment plan should be long-term survival through the preservation of principal.

2. The second goal should be steady growth of capital and/or income.
3. The third and least important goal should be to achieve the highest possible profits.

Most traders put the third goal first and are not even aware of the first two goals. If you do this, you will most probably lose some or all of your capital.

So, let us examine how we go about achieving these goals. If we understand the wonderful results that can be achieved through consistently applying the benefits of compound interest, then we have a foundation on which to build our investment goals.

CHAPTER 3

The Miracle of Compound Interest

> Who told you it cannot be done? What great achievement has he to his credit that entitles him to use the word "impossible" so freely?
> —**Napoleon Hill**

I previously mentioned that I worked in the investment department of a large financial institution. One of the fascinating things about this job was that I had the good fortune to meet so many interesting and successful people. One man I had the good fortune of knowing, Gordon, was in his early forties. He was always coming into the bank dressed in his casual clothes and either depositing or withdrawing large amounts of money. He would sometimes speak briefly to me and then say, "Well, I need to get moving, because I don't want to be late for my golf game." His suntan in the winter always made him appear as though he had recently returned from Florida or the Caribbean. I assumed that he was a member of a wealthy family and had inherited his money, but later I learned that he was not. He had grown up in a low- to middle-income neighborhood not far from the bank location where I worked. Finally, one day I had the opportunity to ask him what he did to accumulate the money necessary to live the lifestyle that he enjoyed, apparently without having to work at a job. He laughed and said, "It's all in the miracle of understanding compound interest. Some people are happy to buy bank certificates of deposit or corporate bonds and make four percent per year on their money. If I can change this into four percent per *month*, then I can make more money in one year than most people make in an entire decade!"

> **Covered Call:** A short position in a call contract that is offset or hedged by a long position in the underlying stock or other asset.

> **Compound or Compound Interest:** The effect that arises when earned interest is added to principal, so that from that moment on, the interest that has been added *itself* earns interest. This addition of interest to the principal is called *compounding* (in other words, the interest is compounded).

I did not learn until many years later, after I had become his frequent golfing partner, that he was simply selling **covered calls** against his stock portfolio.

He had developed a system which he followed religiously. He carried out this investment plan every month by following a specific set of rules regarding when to purchase, when to sell, and when to roll his sold call contracts up, down, or into the next month. By withdrawing less money from his account than he was making every month, he was letting the profits accumulate and **compound**. If you are using this process, then you can accumulate a great fortune over a period of time. The investment guru Warren Buffet has called compounding the "greatest miracle in the world." See the examples below in order to obtain a better understanding of this concept.

It took me years to talk my friend into teaching me his secret formula. He was afraid that if too many people were aware of it, it wouldn't work anymore. Fortunately, this has not proven to be the case. The options markets have grown substantially over the last several decades to the point that no one investor can have much influence on them. We later worked together to refine this process into one that can easily be taught to anyone. I am setting some of these principals out in this book. Others that are more complicated, I teach in my seminars and occasionally in one-on-one mentoring sessions.

Let compound interest work in your favor

Anyone can understand the mathematics of compound interest, but have you ever taken the time to really analyze some examples of compounding and how to use it in your favor? Let's examine what it can do for you.

In setting your investment plan, let the monthly compounding of the return on your money be your most important goal. As we develop our specific investment purchase and sell rules, we will often refer back to this statement as the core of our monthly decision making process. There are two rules to this type of trading. First, do not get careless—be sure to

> **In setting your investment plan, let the monthly compounding of the return on your money be your most important goal.**

make your 3–5 percent per month; second, do not get greedy and shoot for the stars—make your 3–5 percent per month. Yes, the first rule is the same as the second rule, only from the opposite perspective—so remember it!

Set your income goal at 3–5 percent per month

When you follow the 3–5 percent per month rule, you are disciplining yourself to invest rather than speculate. Therefore, embed this important principle in your mind, and don't let it ever escape.

Let's examine the 3–5 percent rule:

- If you can make 3 percent per month, that compounds to 42 percent per year.
- If you can make 5 percent per month, that compounds to 80 percent per year.

I recommend that you set these percentage returns as a goal range that you strive to achieve *every* month. Of course, there will be rough months when you do not achieve these goals, but do not let these bad months destroy your focus of setting and trying to achieve this goal for each and every month. Keep your mind focused on these investment parameters and do not get tempted to make an excessively larger return. It is not necessary to aim higher than the above numbers!

Doing so can lead you into speculative investments or the use of techniques that will only set your account backward instead of forward. Later in this book, we will examine how to set up trades that are designed to achieve these goals.

Let's look at a compound interest example using the 3–5 percent rule.

At a 3 percent per month return on investment, a $25,000 account will perform as follows*:

Year	Amount
Beginning	$25,000
2	50,000
4	100,000
6	200,000
8	400,000
10	800,000
12	1,600,000

*The returns listed above assume that the account is free from federal and state income taxes, as is the case in an IRA, Roth IRA, or 401(k) account.

At 3 percent per month, a standard IRA account with $25,000 will grow to $1,600,000 without additional contributions in twelve years. While these returns are not standard for most investors, they are a goal for which you can be shooting. If you employ the teachings of this course, then you can make this a realistic goal. In real-life investing, there will be setbacks and some losing months, but it is vitally important to always set your goals and rules.

Always write down the rules of the trade

Your rules will change from time to time with the economy and with your level of experience, but you must remember to never change your rules *during* a trade. Prior to opening any and every position, you must write down your rules of the trade, and then *follow your rules*.

One of my mentors used to always require me to say before entering any trade, "The rules are the rules, because they are the rules! Always follow the rules."

Obviously any investment manager that achieved these returns on a consistent basis would be in great demand. You must be wondering, *How can I achieve these results, when some of the best money managers in the world can't do it?*

> **Why can you, an average retail investor, be successful in this endeavor, when most wealthy investment advisors and hedge fund managers who have tremendous resources and research dollars at their disposal cannot? The answer is that we can do so *because* we have small amounts of money to place.**

Why can you, an average retail investor, be successful in this endeavor, when most wealthy investment advisors and hedge fund managers who have tremendous resources and research dollars at their disposal cannot? The answer is that we can do so because we have small amounts of money to place. It is possible to establish or dispose of meaningful positions in a $1 million account quickly and without too much slippage or change in prices. Doing so in a $1 *billion* account is a very different matter. Establishing a meaningful position in an account of this size must usually be done only over a period of weeks or months. During this time, prices and circumstances can change by a considerable amount. In other words, the charting and technical analysis methods taught in this book enable us to detect their expensive research and knowledge and act on it when their capital inflows first begin to drive prices up or down. Because we have small accounts, little overhead, and no lengthy decision-making process, we can act quickly and keep our profits.

The Rule of 72

The Rule of 72 is a common shortcut formula that can be used to determine how long it takes for your account to double in value. It is calculated by dividing your percentage **return on investment** into 72. The result is the

> **Return on Investment:** The profit or loss resulting from a financial transaction divided by the cost of such a transaction. This is usually calculated or expressed as a percentage at an annual rate.

amount of time required to double your money. For example, if you earn 10 percent per annum, then you will double your money in 7.2 years. If you earn 20 percent per annum, then you will double your account value every 3.6 years.

- Later in this book, we will look at the income strategy called "selling covered calls," in which you should consider trying to achieve a return equal to 3–5 percent per month.

- If you earn 4 percent per month, you will double your money every year and a half! (Seventy-two divided by 4 percent per month equals eighteen months.)

- If your account earns 3 percent per month, then it should double every two years. (Seventy-two divided by 3 percent equals twenty-four months.)

CHAPTER 4

Achieve Your Dreams

> All our dreams can come true, if we have
> the courage to pursue them.
> —**Walt Disney**

You can achieve your dreams

Think to yourself for a moment about why you are studying this book. Each one of you has your own reasons for studying this material and your own investment goals and objectives. First of all, let me congratulate you because, by reading this, you have taken step number one in determining the outcome of your family's financial future. The first thing you must do is take your financial future into your own hands, and not leave it to fate. Whether you are an experienced investor or a first-timer, you can improve your investing decisions by taking advantage of the material in this book.

Goal-setting is necessary

Step 1:

If you expect success, then you must first prepare for success. In order for this material to be effective, you need to determine your goals and write them down. On the space provided below, write down in this book why you are studying this material and what you hope to accomplish by mastering the techniques specified in this book. Be specific! Making money is not a specific enough goal. Think about specific things that this money will do for you. For example, do you need to secure your retirement? Do you want to travel? Do you need to replace lost income or have more free time? Do you need to provide for your children's education? Do you need a new car? Do you want to inspire your children, grandchildren, or other family members to learn how to manage their money? *Write your goals now!*

Goal #1:

_____
_____
_____
_____
_____

Goal #2:

_____
_____
_____
_____
_____

Goal #3:

_____
_____
_____
_____

You know your own investment returns in the past. You are probably not too happy with them or else you would not be reading this book. Maybe you are new to investing and have no past performance upon which to base your original goals. This is okay; everyone has to start somewhere. You will not finish this material ready to go and expertly apply the things that are taught herein. You will have to study them over and over and gain experience in using them. Your most important goal should be to always get better!

In time, by applying the principals of this book, experience and understanding will potentially lead to higher returns on your money and better results than you have ever thought possible!

Step 2:
Write down what you see for yourself in the future as a result of reading this book and implementing these investing principles. Post these written goals where you will see them every day. Be specific! After you determine this new future for yourself and your family, you need to envision yourself in this new environment. See yourself there in your subconscious mind and in your dreams and believe in it. Write it now, in the space provided below.

Step 3:

This may be the most important step. Identify what it is in the past that has stopped you from reaching your financial goals. Do you believe that money is easy or difficult to make? Have you traded time for money all of your life or do you make your money work for you? Write these answers below now!

Step 4:

Write down exactly how you intend to let the tools and information from this book and the seminar that follows it help you to achieve your goals. Go back to the beginning of this book and think about why you are reading this material. Write it down below now.

Maintain a positive attitude

Only you can determine your future.

In trading and investing, as in life, your attitude will determine whether or not you are successful. Only with the proper attitude can you use the tools of this book to work through difficulties and reach your goals. To be successful, you need to do the following:

- Have knowledge of the correct tools.
- Obtain the correct training.
- Have the right mental attitude. (If you treat investing as a hobby, then it will pay [cost] you as a hobby! If you treat investing as a business, then it can pay you as a business!)
- Think about running a business and compare it to your investing activities.

Have a trading plan

Before you make any investment, answer to yourself and write down your trading plan, which should include the following:

- Why are you buying or selling a particular stock or option?
- What is your plan or level of profit or loss that you seek to attain?
- What is the long-term trend?
- What are the weekly and daily trends?
- What are the technical indicators showing?

- Did you place your **stop loss order** immediately after the trade was executed?
- What size position can you afford to buy?
- What is your target price or proposed return on investment?
- Is this an income or a speculative trade?
- What is your desired holding time?
- Are there any other things unique to this trade that you should consider?

Stop Loss Order: An order that directs the brokerage firm to automatically exit a position based upon the occurrence of a certain event. This event is usually related to the achievement of a price level of the security or, in the case of a derivative, the price level of the underlying security. This is a sell order in the case of a long position and a buy order in the case of a short position.

Don't worry if some of these terms do not make sense to you at this point. They will be explained as we get into specific income strategies.

Keeping good records—the best sign of success

Just as in any business, you must keep a written record of all of the above, including the gain/loss on every transaction. Also keep written notes as to what you would do differently the next time you enter into a trade such as this one. You should keep a loose-leaf notebook and retain all of your records. Also, you should develop a spreadsheet and record all of your transactions in it. Trading and investing is your business—treat it like a business rather than a hobby!

CHAPTER 5

Save Money through Smart Account Opening

> If thou wouldst keep money, save money; if thou wouldst reap money, sow money.
> —**Thomas Fuller**

Different types of accounts

Almost all brokerage firms allow you to open an account either as an individual, a corporation, an LLC, a joint account, a tenants-by-the-entirety account, or an IRA account. You can fund it initially with cash or with stocks from another account.

> **Margin:** A loan from a brokerage firm to its account holder that is made in order to acquire a larger position than permitted by the available cash in the account. Regulation T of the Securities and Exchange Commission determines the amount or loan to value ratio that can be extended. This ratio changes from time to time.

35

You should always specify that you desire a "margin account." A **margin** account allows you to borrow funds from the brokerage house. Please note that you don't have to **exercise** this right to borrow, but you should have it in case you ever need or want it.

> **Exercise:** Putting into effect an option holder's rights to buy or sell an underlying security at a specific strike price.

You should always complete the options agreement in order that you are permitted to trade options in your account. Depending on your prior experience, you will be permitted to carry out certain transactions. If your brokerage company is too restrictive, then you need to consider switching to a different firm. You will usually be asked most of the following questions:

- What amount of funds do you have available for trading?
- How many years of investment experience do you have?
- What is the level of your investment knowledge?
- What is the average size of your past transactions?
- What is the average number of transactions per year?
- What is the average size of each transaction?
- What type of securities have you traded (stocks, bonds, options, etc.)?
- What are your investment objectives?
- What are the types of activities that you plan to transact in your account?

It is very important that you understand that these questions are *not* designed to help or protect you! They are to protect the brokerage firm. Many independent advisors recommend that you fill out the form in such a manner as to achieve the maximum amount of flexibility on your behalf.

Lower your commissions

There are many reputable brokerage firms, both national and regional. You will want to investigate their financial stability as well as the level of commissions that they will charge you. If you are a trader or an active investor, then you do *not* want to do business with a full service broker. Remember—you care about your net return after commissions, slippage, and other charges. There are also online discount brokers. Some discount brokerage firms with which you are probably familiar are Schwab, TD Ameritrade, E*Trade, Fidelity, and many others. While these firms are certainly reputable, they are not set up to handle the activities of customers that are active traders and that deal in options. They do not offer or make the tools available that you will need in order to make informed investment decisions. This is especially true if you move on from the basic strategies taught in this book to more advanced methods of income trading that can be learned at seminars available through www.incomestrategiesacademy.com.

Avoid "trade for a hobby" brokerage firms

Some brokerage firms that *do* have income trading tools available to clients are optionsXpress, Optionetics, optionMONSTER, and thinkorswim (a subsidiary of TD

Ameritrade). It may take you a great deal of time to learn a brokerage firm's trading platform, but it can be done. You should spend the time necessary to do it. There are seminars available on this subject. Most of these options specialists firms are headquartered in Chicago. Most of the traders and officers of these firms were formerly market makers, specialists, or traders at the CBOE or another options exchange. They are traders themselves, and they understand what platform and information traders need in order to be successful. Some of the exhibits in this book were reprinted from the thinkorswim platform. You will not be able to analyze advanced non-directional income trades without access to an options platform, as well as to charts that have the capability to evaluate your positions and the effect of adjustments that are made to these positions after the trade is opened.

You *cannot* do sophisticated investing on a "trading for a hobby" brokerage platform.

CHAPTER 6

Make Easy Money by Understanding Indexes and ETFs

> Money and time are the heaviest burdens in life, and the unhappiest of all mortals are those who have more of either than they know how to use.
> —**Samuel Johnson**

In order to start an income trade, you will need to choose the underlying investment vehicle. This short chapter examines some of the possible choices. It is important to remember that we are *not* looking to make our monthly income or return on this underlying security. We make the monthly income through the time value deterioration of the option that we sell against it. In choosing a trading vehicle, we desire a stable, liquid security that trades at least one million shares each day.

Avoid mutual funds

Because of their diversified base, high liquidity, and stability, some people prefer to own a portfolio of stocks through the purchase of mutual funds.

Mutual funds are characterized by the following traits:

- High management fees
- Sometimes high entry and exit fees
- Do not offer options
- Cannot be shorted or otherwise hedged
- Can only be bought or sold at the end of a trading day.

For these reasons, I do not recommend investing in mutual funds. *They are generally good only for the investment managers who take the high fees from managing them.*

Index investing—low commissions and broad diversification

If you want to diversify across a broad spectrum of stocks without incurring the pitfalls and high fees of investing in mutual funds, then you can invest in an exchange traded fund or ETF that mirrors an Index.

Some of the most liquid of these are listed later in this chapter.

You can also invest directly in an index by investing in their calls and puts. The S&P 500 Index, which has the symbol SPX, is the most broadly diversified and actively traded index in the world. You can own it (later we will see how a synthetic ownership position can be created with options) without any fees except an entry and exit commission. You can also simulate a **long position** in it by buying calls or a **short position** by buying puts. Later in this book, we will also show you how to create a synthetic covered-call position in order to generate a monthly income using an Index.

The Indexes with the most actively traded options are as follows:

- SPX—S&P 500
- NDX—**NASDAQ** 100
- RUT—Russell 2000
- DJX—Dow Jones 1/100 Mini
- MNX—Mini NASDAQ 100
- OEX—S&P 100 Index

> **NASDAQ:** The National Association of Securities Dealers Automated Quotations is a computerized system that allows brokers and dealers to get quotes and to trade the stocks that qualify to be listed.

By investing in **index options**, you avoid paying any management fees at all. Commissions are low, synthetic shorting is possible, and indexes have actively traded and highly liquid options.

> **Index Options:** Call and put options in an underlying index.

Index options are one of the primary ways to take advantage of option investing. Options on the primary indices have the following characteristics that are necessary for successful option trading:

1. High volume
2. Ease of entry and exit at a mid-price or halfway between the bid and asked prices (this results in reduced slippage)
3. No company or industry earnings risk
4. No company-specific news risk or CEO risk
5. Lower implied volatility than most common stocks
6. High visibility
7. Possible tax advantages (see your tax advisor for information on possible capital gain treatment from short-term trading in index options; Section 1256 of the IRC).
8. They are cash settled as opposed to being settled with a distribution of securities, as are ETFs.

We will discuss index option trading strategies in more depth later in this book.

The advantages of investing in ETFs

ETFs (Exchange Traded Funds) offer the same advantages as do the indexes (except tax), and they should be considered as a viable part of any investment strategy. Index ETFs, which are also called index tracking stocks, are similar to mutual funds in that they are a basket of stocks. A basket of stocks simply means that many stocks are thrown into the mix of holdings, or basket. However, they charge much lower management fees than do most mutual funds. Some of the most heavily traded index-related ETFs are as follows:

- DIA: Dow Jones 30
- QQQQ: NASDAQ 100
- SPY: S&P 500
- EWJ: Japan Index
- IWM: Russell 2000
- XLF: Finance Sector
- XLE: Energy Sector

Advantages of ETFs over Mutual Funds are as follows:

> **Long Position:** If a stock or other position is owned, one is said to be long in it.

> **Short Position:** A position in a security wherein it has been sold, but it has not yet been bought. In order to close out this transaction, this security must be purchased. One would desire to be short if he believed that the value of the security will decline.

- Trade like stocks during the entire trading day
- Can be sold short
- No front-end or back-end load fees
- Most are optionable

You can trade an ETF at any time the markets are open. You can buy or sell short an ETF. You can employ covered-call selling and other options strategies when using an ETF. You should consider making the ownership of ETFs an important part of your investment program, especially while you are learning to trade. Positions in Index ETFs can be established for much less cash consideration per share than positions in indexes. Positions in Index ETFs have tight bid-ask spreads and result in small slippage, but their smaller price per share results in higher commissions.

CHAPTER 7

Selecting and Timing Your Stock Purchases

> Fear always springs from ignorance.
> —**Ralph Waldo Emerson**

It would be difficult to produce consistent income through the use of non-directional income trading techniques without first learning some of the basics about when to buy into a position and when to sell out of a position. After all, if you make a profit of 3–5 percent per month on your income trade, but lose twice that much on your underlying position, then you have suffered a setback, not a gain.

Defining price

Before we analyze price entry and exit point strategies, let's think for a minute about the definition of price. Can you define price? Here are some answers that I have read or heard about in the past.

Price:

- Perceived value
- The amount that one person will pay for a given commodity at a given point in time
- The amount of the last trade
- The amount one can get for something at this exact moment in time
- The amount that the *next* person will pay

What if there is no bid? Then what is the price? Think about mortgage derivatives in the 2008–2009 market. What is the value of a product that has no bid?

> **Bid Price:** The offered price by market makers or an exchange to buy a stock, index, or option.

> **Ask Price:** The lowest price that a seller on an exchange will accept for securities or other assets at a given moment in time.

Prices on stock and option exchanges have a **bid price** and an **ask price**. If no one steps in the middle, then there is no price. Price is the intersection of the demand and supply curves. Each price represents a momentary consensus of value between buyers, sellers, and undecided traders at the moment of the transaction. There is always a crowd of traders behind each side of every transaction.

In normal business transactions between corporations, both big and small, it is common for companies to help each other. This is true, because by helping your suppliers and customers, you are helping yourself. However, the stock market is a business wherein every player tries to take money away from every other trader. Unlike other businesses, in the stock market, everyone else is against you! This includes your broker, the market makers, exchange specialists, and anyone else who has a conflict of interest between themselves and your money. No one is helping out the other guy. Not only are you competing against some of the brightest minds in the world, but you are fighting off the enemies of commissions and slippage.

Prices are defined by a crowd mentality. It is this market psychology that makes markets work efficiently. This price action is the basis of **technical analysis**.

> **Technical Analysis:** A method of evaluating and forecasting the future price of a security by observing and measuring certain mathematical relationships between past price movement, volume, and volatility.

Technical analysis—one of the keys to success

What is technical analysis? Technical analysis is the application of market assessments based upon social psychology. Its goal is to recognize trends and changes in crowd behavior in order to make intelligent trading decisions. This recognition attempt is to enable one to trade before news becomes public knowledge, and to do it without having illegal insider knowledge.

Learning to properly apply basic technical analysis can be your edge in beating the crowd in the game of investing in stocks and options.

Why technical analysis works

Large hedge funds and other income generators like Warren Buffet's Berkshire Hathaway have huge portfolios of stocks against which they generate income by writing call options. Since I assume that you are not fortunate enough to hold such a large portfolio (or else you wouldn't be taking the time to read this), I'll begin by going over the process of choosing which stocks to use as core holdings. In the first part of this book, I discussed the desired holding period for day trading, income trading, and buy-and-hold investing. Since we are focusing on *monthly* income, we will also focus on our average holding period being equal to one month. If a holding turns out to be much longer, then that is good, but we won't count on it.

> **It is very important to understand that anything investment managers tell us on a financial television show or in a financial newspaper is for their benefit, not ours.**

Many large mutual and hedge funds invest billions of dollars. They have unlimited money to spend analyzing the various sectors, industries, and companies in which to invest. They have large research staffs, direct access to corporate officers, and sometimes even seats on corporate boards of directors. They know more than you or I, as retail traders, will ever know. We cannot compete with them using the process of fundamental analysis. It is very important to understand that anything investment managers tell us on a financial television show or in a financial newspaper is for their benefit, not ours. In other words, if an analyst or money manager opines on television or in a financial newspaper to buy the stock of a particular company, then you can

> **Unlike other businesses, in the stock market, everyone else is against you!**

be rest assured that their fund has already finished buying it, and is even probably selling it by now. *They need buyers to whom to sell!*

A retail investor, like you or me, must learn how to buy a stock at the same time that the institutions are *beginning* to accumulate it. Because we cannot afford to do this through conducting our own fundamental research, we must learn how to read charts and perform technical analysis. You can start your own stock selection process by going over some of the simple basics of these procedures.

Trend following your way to profits

You may have heard the saying, "The trend is your friend." This statement is true! Do not trade against the trend or else you will probably lose some of your money. Of course, this flies directly against the typical fundamentalist or value investor viewpoint. Fundamentalist money managers and analysts normally recommend companies and industries when the stocks are down. They refer to these stocks as being "undervalued." The truth is that these stocks are down because of a reason that may not yet be known to the general public. Charting and technical analysis can reveal that there is a problem, although it will not necessarily reveal what the problem is. You can then act upon this knowledge before it's too late.

Charting—a way to "forecast" future price movements

Your brokerage firm's trading platform should have charting services available to all customers as a part of its normal service. The web site www.freestockcharts.com also allows you to access free stock charts and to superimpose technical analysis indicators and trend lines upon them. If you want to learn the methods of how to do your own charting, then you can learn to do so at one of my income trading seminars, which can be found at www.incomestrategiesacademy.com.

The chart on Exhibit 1 is a nineteen-month daily graph of Potash Company from January 2007–August 2008. The solid black line is the trend line. Notice that the stock price bounced off of this trend line many times during its one-and-a-half-year run-up in price. These bounce points were the times to buy, or the entry points. You should not sell a stock short with a rising trend line. When a stock is in an uptrend, it will usually bounce off of the support trend line many times on its way up.

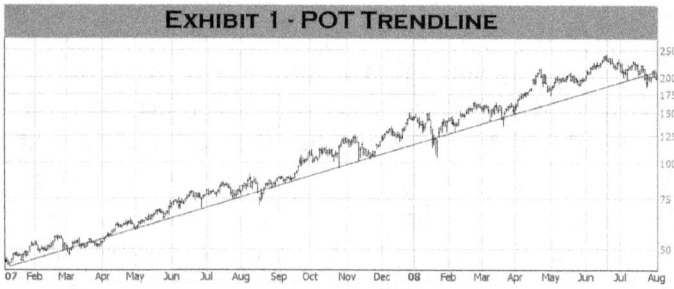

An uptrend exists when there are higher highs and higher lows. A downtrend exists when there are lower highs and lower lows. You should draw trend lines on a chart of any stock that you are considering trading. When you are doing your own charting, you should always use a logarithm scale. You should never trade or fight *against* the trend; you should always trade with the trend. If an uptrend reverses and there is a lower high and a lower low, then it is time to exit the trade and perhaps to sell the stock short. If a downtrend reverses and there is a higher high and a higher low, then it is time to cover your short position and to perhaps go long.

The solid line in Exhibit 2 illustrates a two-and-one-half-year downtrend in Citigroup Company from June 2006 until November 2008. Notice that the trend remained intact throughout this entire time frame, although it did change its slope in June 2007. When a stock is in a downtrend, it will usually bounce off the resistance trend line (or close to it) many times on its downward journey.

The rules of trend following:

- Draw your own trend lines in order to plot your course of action.
- Always draw trend lines with a broad paintbrush, rather than with a fine pencil.

- Do not buy stocks that are in a downtrend.
- Do not sell short stocks that are in an uptrend.
- Buy stocks that are in an uptrend when they are bouncing off of their trend support line.
- Sell or sell short stocks that are in a downtrend when they are bouncing off their resistance line.
- Always draw diagonal trend lines as well as horizontal support and resistance lines. Let these lines, together with technical indicators, be your guide as to when and at what price to buy or to place stop orders.
- Always look for the formation of a channel, which is the area that lies between the support and the resistance lines in both trending markets and stable markets.

Support and resistance

If you throw a rubber ball down, it will hit the floor and bounce up. If it hits the ceiling, then it will bounce down. Support and resistance are to stock prices what the floor and ceiling are to the ball.

Support is a price level at which buying is strong enough to reverse a downtrend. When a downtrend hits support, it bounces like that ball when it hits the floor.

Resistance is a price level at which sellers become strong enough to reverse an uptrend. When an uptrend hits resistance, it reverses like that ball when it hits the ceiling.

It is better to draw support and resistance lines across *congested areas* rather than at the extreme price levels. Traders buy at support and sell at resistance, thus making their effectiveness a self-fulfilling prophecy. The greater the volume or number of shares traded in a congested area, the stronger and more reliable it is. Support and resistance areas exist because people have memories. This is an example of social psychology at work in the financial markets.

Trend lines and moving averages can provide support and resistance points as a stock moves in one direction. Support and resistance can also be provided via horizontal lines. A stock's past price movement determines certain levels above or below which a psychological price barrier exists. Stocks do not generally pierce these barriers unless there is a significant change in fundamentals or events.

If a stock does break through a support or resistance level on high volume, it is usually a signal that a reversal will occur and that a large price movement in that direction may be anticipated. This somewhat unusual occurrence is referred to as a "breakout." If you can read a breakout and act on it with a directional trade, large profits can result. If you attempt this tactic, use tight sell-stop points in order to protect yourself against a reversal or **regression to the mean**.

Exhibit 3 illustrates a weekly chart of the price movement of McDonalds Corp stock from 2005 until 2010. You can see the solid trendline that is a support bottom from 2005 until October 2008, and then becomes a resistance line until January 2009. It changes from a support line into a resistance line in

> **Regression to the Mean:** A statistical term which refers to the fact that things usually return to normal or the way that they were before. In reference to financial pricing, this means that prices do not generally move more than one standard deviation, based upon historical volatility, before they reverse course and head back to their prior average.

November 2008. Channeling lines run from 2008 through 2009. At the far right edge of this chart, this stock remains in a firm two-and-one-half-year channel. Any breakout of this channel, if accompanied with large volume, will probably indicate a directional opportunity.

Put the odds in your favor

Later, we will see how placing bets on **option spreads** above and below these support and resistance lines can put the odds of winning in your favor. By using these charting methods, you can greatly improve the odds of placing a winning trade. You can never *always* win, but if you put the odds in your favor, then your chance of long-term success is greatly enhanced.

Technical indicators

There are more technical analysis tools than anyone would ever want to know about, much less try to follow. If you try to follow too many indicators, you will just confuse yourself. In this book, we will go over a few of the basic technical indicators that can be most helpful in determining buy and sell points and entry and exit timing. It is my belief that sticking to the basics of technical analysis can make you a winner, just as sticking to the basics of blocking and tackling can lead to winning in football. If one tries to make things too complicated, he usually fools no one but himself.

It is necessary to use a charting service that has computer-generated tools in order to make accurate analyses in an efficient amount of time. There are many such services available. If your brokerage firm does not provide this service free of charge, then you should consider another firm. If you do not want to use a different brokerage firm, then you can find free charting services at www.freestockcharts.com or you can purchase a slightly more sophisticated charting service named "ProphetCharts," which can be purchased at www.prophet.net. ProphetCharts is owned by TD Ameritrade.

Moving averages

Moving averages are the most commonly used tool in determining the direction of the trend and the points of support and resistance. Many people start out in charting by letting moving average graphs identify the trend. A moving average is simply an average of the closing prices over the number of days being measured. Each day, the oldest price is removed and the most recent price is added; the sum is then divided by the number of days being measured. The most commonly used moving average is the thirty-day moving average. However, the fifty-day and the two-hundred-day moving averages are frequently used also. You should always place several different time frames of moving averages on any chart that is examined.

> **Option Spread:** A simultaneous purchase and sell of two different options in hope that the difference between their prices (the spread) will accrue to the benefit of the investor as either the price of the underlying security changes or the time value of the two options evaporates.

The most important thing to notice about the moving average is the direction of its slope. If you have a problem determining the direction, just imagine that you place a marble on the moving average line. The direction that it rolls determines the trend. If it rolls back in time, the trend is up. If it rolls forward in time, the direction is down.

> **Exponential Moving Average (EMA):** An average of past prices that is weighted to give greater influence to the most recent data. It therefore responds faster to changing input.

A variation of moving average that is an even better trend-following tool is the **exponential moving average (EMA)**. It gives greater weight to the latest data and therefore responds to changes faster than a simple moving average. EMA does not respond to old data as much as does a simple moving average.

I will not get into the technicalities of computing EMA or any of the other technical indicators that we will examine. That exercise is fine for mathematicians and engineers, but it is not necessary in order to make money as a trader. In order to make money, you need only to know how to use these tools.

I like to frequently use the thirty-day MA and the thirteen-day EMA on my daily charts. These provide insight that is good enough for our simple analysis. Exhibit 4 is a chart of the S&P 500 Index from February 2007 to December of 2009. The chart contains a thirteen-day EMA line and thirty-day MA line. Notice first the slope of the lines. Also notice that when the faster moving thirteen-day EMA line crosses above the slower thirty-day line, it's time to buy or "go long," and when it crosses below the slower moving average, it's time to sell or "go short."

It is important to notice that the thirteen-day EMA serves as a line of support at some times and a line of resistance at others.

MACD: The strongest indicator of future price movement

Moving averages filter out daily price inconsistencies and give a trend line. MACD, which stands for moving average convergence and divergence ("Mac Dee"), consists of three exponential moving averages. They appear on charts as two lines whose crossovers give trading signals. The most commonly used MACD is calculated as follows:

1. Calculate the twelve-day and twenty-six-day exponential moving averages (EMA) of closing prices.

2. Subtract the twenty-six-day from the twelve-day EMA to obtain the fast line.
3. Calculate a nine-day EMA of this fast line. It will give you the slow signal line.
4. Plot both lines to obtain the classic MACD indicator.
5. Subtract the signal line from the MACD line to obtain the MACD Histogram.

Note: It is best to use the standard twelve/twenty-six/nine MACD Histogram unless you become an expert on this tool and develop your own method of linking cycles on different time frames.

> **Bull:** An investor that believes that a stock or the general level of the stock market is expected to rise.

> **Bear:** An investor that believes that a stock or the market is expected to fall.

In my opinion, MACD Histogram is the single best tool available to market technicians. It offers an insight into whether the **bulls** or the **bears** are in control of the market and also an indication as to whether their strength is growing stronger or weaker. If the fast line is above the slow line, then MACD Histogram is positive. If the fast line is below the slow line, then MACD Histogram is negative. When the two lines touch, then MACD Histogram is equal to zero. If the spread between the two lines increases, then MACD Histogram becomes taller or deeper. The slope of the MACD Histogram is determined by the relationship between the two most recent bars.

Important note: do not trade against the slope of the weekly MACD Histogram.

You will want to observe MACD Histogram in several different time frames in order to make buying decisions that are in accordance with maximizing your probability of profit. This is done by alternating between daily and weekly charts.

> **Important note: do not trade against the slope of the *weekly* MACD Histogram.**
>
> **In order to make money, you need only to know how to use these tools.**

Exhibit 5 is a daily chart of the Russell 2000 Index from December 2006–December 2008. MACD histogram is shown on the chart below the graph. Please note that when the *slope* of this MACD Histogram changes, it usually indicates that a change of price direction will follow.

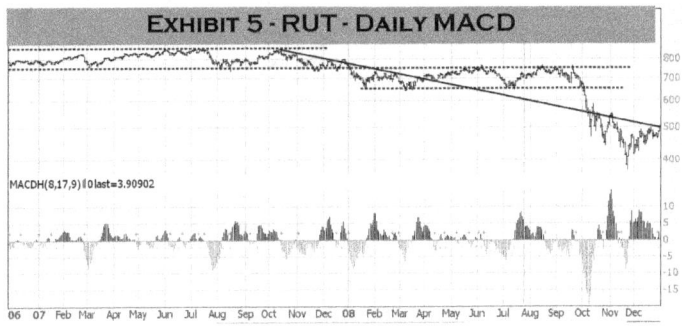

Exhibit 6 is a weekly chart of the Russell 2000 Index. Focus on the change in the *slope* of MACD Histogram as it relates to the channeling index and the future changes in price. Also note that, in addition to the MACD Histogram, the MACD lines are plotted on this graph. The crossover of the lines can occur while the MACD remains at a very high or a very low level. Thus, it is important to note that a change in the weekly MACD slope can be a very valuable tool in predicting future price changes.

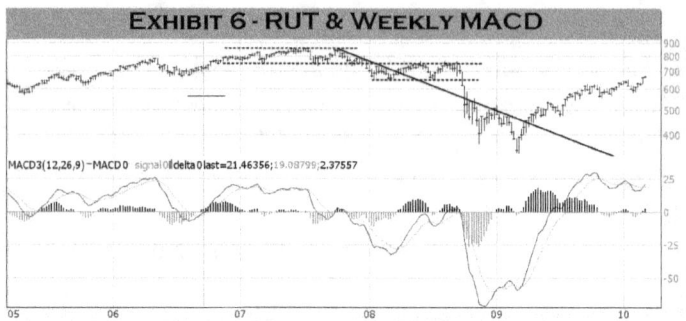

Stochastic—the timing indicator

Stochastic is a technical measurement of the relationship of closing prices to the recent high–low range. The standard width of a stochastic time window is five days. You do not need to know how to calculate stochastic, but, you *do* need to know how to read the stochastic graph and how to apply the rules to a trade. When using stochastic:

1. There are two measures of stochastic; these are the fast stochastic and the slow stochastic. Use the slow stochastic option. Fast stochastic changes too quickly, and the use of it can lead you into following whipsaws.

2. A five-bar stochastic smoothed over a three-day time frame is the recommended setting.

3. Stochastic is designed to fluctuate between 0 and 100 percent. Reference lines are usually drawn at 20 per-

cent and 80 percent in order to indicate overbought and oversold market conditions.

Remember that each price or transaction is the consensus of all traders' opinions at the exact moment of the transaction. Daily closing prices are more important than daily price ranges, because the settlement of trading accounts depends on them. The high of any period marks the maximum power of the bulls during that time. The low of any period marks the maximum power of the bears during that time.

Stochastic marks the ability of the bulls or bears to close the market at the upper or lower edge of the recent range. When prices rally, markets tend to close near the daily high. If the bulls can raise prices during the day, but cannot close them near the high, then stochastic turns down. It shows that bulls are weaker than they seem and gives a sell signal.

An upturn of stochastic shows that the bears have run out of power and that an upturn in prices is likely. *Use stochastic as a timing device only*; do not use it to make a buy or sell decision.

- Do not buy when stochastic is overbought (above 80 percent).
- Do not sell short when stochastic is oversold (below 20 percent).

Exhibit 7 shows a stochastic indicator chart below a daily price chart of the Russell 2000 Index.

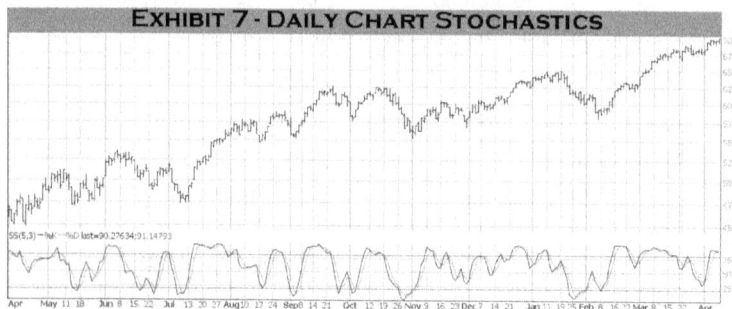

Stochastic is normally viewed only on a daily chart because it's a timing tool rather than a decision-making tool, as is the MACD.

The Elder-Ray Indicator

The Elder-Ray Indicator was developed in 1989 by Dr. Alexander Elder, a well known directional trader and instructor. He believes that, just as doctors use X rays to see below the surface of the skin, traders can use the Elder-Ray to see below the surface of the markets. You only need to find when the bulls or the bears are in control and then trade with the dominant group.

Bull Power is the high of the day minus the thirteen-day EMA.

Bear Power is the low of the day minus the thirteen-day EMA.

It is normal for Bull Power to be positive and for Bear Power to be negative. The higher the Bull Power, the stronger the buying power of the bulls. The lower the Bear Power, the stronger the selling power of the bears. Elder-Ray compares the maximum power of the bulls and the bears to push the average consensus of value. It does this by measuring the spread between the high and the low of every bar and an EMA.

Rules of Elder Ray:

- Buy only if
    - The trend of both indicators is up
    - Bear Power is negative but rising
- Sell or sell short only if
    - The trend of both indicators is down
    - Bull Power is positive but falling
- Do not buy if
    - Both the bull line and the bear line are positive—the market is overbought
- Do not sell or sell short if
    - Both the bull line and the bear line are negative—the market is oversold

Exhibit 8 applies an Elder-Ray Indicator to a Russell 2000 chart.

Channeling bands

Prices flow in channels, the way that rivers flow in valleys. When a river touches the rim of its valley, it turns in the other direction. When prices rally, they seem to turn at an invisible ceiling, and when they fall, they seem to hit an invisible floor. Channels help traders identify buying and selling opportunities and avoid bad trades by identifying support and resistance. Channels are constructed in a number of different ways:

1. Draw channel lines parallel to a trend line.
2. Draw channel lines parallel to a moving average.
3. Draw a moving average of the highs and another of the lows.
4. Draw two lines parallel to the EMA with the distance between the two lines changing based on the stock's volatility.

> **Using Bollinger Bands is necessary when comparing the prices of options, because option pricing is based on volatility.**

The channels described in method number four above are referred to as Bollinger Bands. The width between these two lines varies depending on the standard deviation of price changes during the period of measurement. Using Bollinger Bands is necessary when comparing the prices of options, because option pricing is based on volatility. Fortunately, you do not have to calculate and plot Bollinger Bands. Most charting services will do this for you. You should set the width of the bands at 2.0, which is two standard deviations from the mean. Therefore, the channel will envelop a 95 percent probability of the possible price range. Set the time frame for twenty days. This is the average holding time of a one month option.

Bollinger Bands Rules:

- When prices are near the top range of the Bollinger Band, it is time to sell the underlying stock or index, or, if the underlying security is in an uptrend, to sell a call against the position. This strategy will be explained later.

- When prices are near the bottom range of the band, it is time to look at buying the underlying stock or index, or to sell a **naked put** in order to either collect premium if it goes unexercised or to establish a favorable position price if it is exercised.

  > **Naked Put:** A sold or short put position that is not supported by any underlying security or hedge position. The maximum risk is the strike price, if the stock goes to zero.

- If prices are outside of the channel on high volume, look for a possible breakout.

- If prices are outside of the channel on moderate or low volume, look for them to pull back or regress to the mean soon.

Exhibit 9 is a chart of Bollinger Bands on an IBM weekly chart from May 2008 to April 2010.

For practice, examine some charts on your own; try the stocks or indexes listed below.

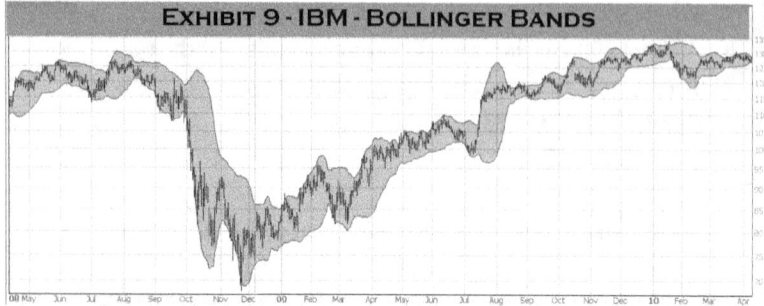

$RUT	JNJ	TLT	XOM	AAPL
$SPX	MCD	T	FCX	RIMM
$NDX	BAX	POT	GLD	MSFT
IWM	KOM	ON	GDX	CSCO
QQQQ	PEP	FXI	EWZ	HPQ
SPY	WMT	VIX	MON	X
IBM	UUP	YUM	MMM	HON

CHAPTER 8

Put the Odds in Your Favor—Use Options

If you hesitate or turn backward while under fire, you are not a fighter—you're a quitter; and the devil himself hates a person with a rubber backbone.
—**Anonymous**

Options defined

Definition: *An option is a contract that gives the owner the right to buy **or** sell a specific asset at a certain price on or before a certain date.*

Most people just beginning to learn about stock options already understand real estate options, but become confused when talking about stock options. So I will start our analysis of options by looking at real estate options.

Limit risk and increase return on investment

Let's say that I want to buy a piece of property that has an agreed-upon value of $100,000. I do not have the money for the down payment at this time, and I know that it will take me some time to arrange for financing. So, I approach the owner and ask him for an option to purchase the property while I am arranging financing. We agree on the price, but the owner will probably next ask me how long a period I need in order to close. He will also expect me to pay an amount of money that is *not* applicable to the purchase price in order to compensate him for the delay (time value) and for the risk that the property may decline in value and I might not close at all. Let's say that I need one year to close and that we agree upon an option price of $10,000, which is 10 percent of the purchase price. If I actually buy the property, then my real cost is $110,000, which is the cost of the option plus the cost of the property at closing.

I now have an option to purchase the property for a period of one year. This option cost me $10,000, and it gives me the right to purchase the property for a price of $100,000. The owner retains the title and all rights to use or rent the property until I pay him and close. Whether I close in one month or in one year, the owner keeps my $10,000; however, the property remains encumbered by my right to purchase it, and he cannot sell it to anyone else until I either buy it or let the option expire. If I do not buy the property during the option period, then the option expires, and the owner keeps my $10,000.

If, during the year, the real estate market crashes, and the property is now worth only $50,000, will I still exercise the option? Of course not! I had an *option* to buy, not an *obligation* to buy. The risk of ownership and of a decline in value remains with the owner. My risk is limited to the $10,000 option price.

On the other hand, what if, during the year, some $1 million homes are built in the neighborhood and the value of the property goes up to $150,000? Now will I close? Yes, I will! I can buy the property and then quickly resell it, for its new current value. Thus, I had a cost of $110,000 and a profit of $40,000. I will make $40,000 divided by $110,000, or a 36 percent return on investment.

What if I still can't come up with the money to close? Then I can sell the option for $50,000. This transaction will also yield me a profit of $40,000, which is the sell price of $50,000 less the $10,000 that I paid for the option. This is a return on investment of 400 percent.

So, the use of an option has limited my risk and increased my return on investment.

There are options to buy (call options) and options to sell (put options). Let's examine the characteristics of each.

Call options

A contract that gives the holder or owner the option to buy an asset is referred to as a call option. It must have three characteristics:

1. A specific price, or **strike price**, at which it is exercisable

    Strike Price: The price at which a call or put option can be exercised.

2. A specific amount of time, or date of **expiration**

3. A specific price, or premium, for the option

    Expiration: The date and time after which an option can no longer be exercised.

The positive difference (if any) between the current market price of the underlying security and the strike price is the intrinsic value. In other words, if I have an option to purchase real estate for $90,000 that is worth $100,000, then the intrinsic (or real) value is $10,000.

The excess amount (if any) between the market value of the underlying security and the strike price is the extrinsic value, or time value premium. In the above real estate example, the option is to buy real estate for $100,000 that is worth $100,000, and we must pay $10,000 for this option. The extrinsic or time value is therefore equal to $10,000. If you own an option to buy something for an amount that is greater than its current value, then that option is said to be "out of the money" and to have no intrinsic value. Therefore, the entire premium is extrinsic value. These out of the money options are usually the options that you will want to sell, especially if you believe that the underlying stock will increase in value. This is the first step in putting the odds in your favor.

The sum of the intrinsic value plus the extrinsic value is equal to the price of the option or the option premium.

Put options

A contract that gives the holder or owner the right to *sell* an asset is referred to as a put option. It must have the same three characteristics as call options: strike price, expiration date, and specific premium.

In the case of a put option, it only has intrinsic or real value if the price at which it is exercisable is *above* the current market price. In other words, if I have the right to sell you a property for $100, 000 while that property is only worth $90,000, then that option contract has intrinsic value equal to $10,000.

Think again about a stock option just as if it is a real estate option. A stock option is just a contract with three parts, as follows:

1. **Strike price**: The price at which the two parties agree to strike a deal. In the real estate example, the strike price is $100,000, which is also the current market value of the property. In dealing with securities, strike prices that are different from the current market value are often used. Strike prices are preset by the options exchanges. They are generally uniform, but may vary depending on the price level and volume of the underlying security.

2. **Date of expiration**: The month in which the option will expire. This is normally the end of business on the third Friday of each month with common stocks and ETFs. It is the *opening* of business on this same Friday in the case of index options.

3. **Premium**: The price or amount of money that exchanges hands in order to buy or sell an option. In the above real estate example, the premium is the $10,000 that is paid for the option.

In order to view these items for any option, look at an options table. These tables are available for free on Yahoo Finance, or you can look in your brokerage firm's platform. Notice that, just

> **Limit Order:** An order that is placed with a maximum price to be paid in the case of a buy, or long position, or a minimum price with respect to a sell, or short position.

like stocks, options have a bid price and an ask price. The spread between these two quotes is usually much larger than the spread on common stocks. Therefore you must always take care to enter **limit orders** only.

Use options to insure your portfolio

When you own a home, you purchase insurance to protect it against the asset losing its value quickly, perhaps due to a fire, flood, or some other catastrophe. That insurance policy allows for someone else to assume this risk for you. In exchange, you pay the insurance company a premium. For a little bit of money now, they will protect the value of your home until the policy's expiration date. At that time, you must pay a new premium in order for them to continue to protect the value of your home for another period of time.

You probably pay thousands of dollars every year in order to insure your home against a catastrophic loss. Do you pay the premium and then hope for a fire to destroy your home? No, you actually hope to lose this premium, rather than to collect on it. Think of insurance on your portfolio in the same way.

Notice the similarities of this example to the put option. The face value of the insurance policy is the strike price. This is the price or amount that you will be paid if a loss occurs. The expiration date identifies the date when the contract between the two parties expires. Lastly, the premium is the amount that you paid to the insurance company, in advance, in order to buy the contract. It is a nonrefundable payment that obligates the company to guarantee the value of the home.

Let's say that you insure your home for its full value of $200,000. If there is no loss, then the company does not have to pay anything at all. However, they will not return your premium payment. This is their cost for assuming the risk of loss.

On the other hand, suppose that a fire occurred and there were $50,000 in damages. The insurance would pay you the amount of the actual loss (less any deductible). They would pay the amount of the loss up to the face value of the policy. In this case, they would pay you 25 percent of the face value. If there is ever a total loss, then they would pay you the full face value amount of $200,000. In other words, the greater the loss, the more the contract is worth.

Let's think about this for a minute. We use insurance for almost every important financial area of our lives. We insure our homes, cars, life, health, etc. *But very few people insure their most valuable asset*—their portfolio or retirement account. They leave it unprotected. This does not make good sense!

Should you have a policy to cover a loss in the value of your portfolio in case of a sudden drop in the market due to an unexpected event such as a terrorist attack or a banking crisis? It happens all too often. In fact, most people do not even know that they can insure themselves against a market crash. You *can* do it. In fact, you are not being prudent if you don't do it!

A put option is a type of insurance. When your house burns down, your insurance company says, "We will *put* it back." The name of the option contract that is used to do the same thing for your retirement portfolio is a put option. It can be a put on certain stocks, if you own a large concentration in certain companies, or a put on a major index in order to protect a broadly diversified portfolio.

> **most people do not even know that they can insure themselves against a market crash.**

A put option on a stock allows you to sell your stock at a price that is guaranteed by the option contract, even if the stock falls to a much lower price by expiration day. In other words, if you buy ABC for thirty-four dollars per share and purchase a put contract to insure it at a thirty-dollar strike price per share, then even if the price drops to twenty dollars or lower, you do not have to be concerned, because you have limited your loss to four dollars per share. You can put it to the seller of the contract at a price equal to thirty dollars. In this case, at a twenty-dollar stock price at the expiration of the option, the option has a value equal to ten dollars per share, which is the difference between the stock price and the strike price of the purchased put contract.

The difference between the current price of a stock and the strike price of an option is referred to as the real or intrinsic value of the option. The exchange is obligated to buy the stock from you at the strike price, because you paid the premium when you bought the put option.

If the stock instead increases in value, then the put option has no value. If the stock is priced above thirty dollars per share at the expiration of the option, then the option has zero value.

Each option contract represents the right to either buy or to sell one hundred shares of stock. It is priced on a per-share basis, so you have to multiply this price by one hundred in order to calculate the actual price of one contract.

Hard Times Easy Trading | 75

In order to help you understand the discussion of options, let's explain some of the most commonly used terms to describe options.

Options terminology

At the money: The stock price and the strike price are roughly the same.

In the money: The option contract has real or intrinsic value if it were exercised today.

Out of the money: The option contract has no real or intrinsic value if it were exercised today.

Bid: The amount required in order sell a stock or an option.

Ask: The amount required in order to buy a stock or an option.

Intrinsic value: The actual cash value of an option, if it is exercised today.

Extrinsic value: The value of an option that is over and above its actual value, if it is exercised today. This is also sometimes referred to as the time value. Some market makers call it juice.

Delta: The change in the price of an option that will occur with a one-point change in the price of the underlying instrument. If a call has a delta of .50, then its price will move up or down by fifty cents when the price of the underlying stock moves up or down by one dollar.

Gamma: The change in the price of an option that will occur with a one-point move in the option's delta. As the gamma increases, the volatility or risk of the position is increased.

Theta: A measurement of the daily rate of depreciation of an option contract's price based upon the assumption that the underlying stock's price and implied volatility remain stagnant. Thus, it is referring to the loss in value that is due to time or extrinsic value depreciation.

Vega: The change in the price of an option that is due to a change in the implied volatility of the underlying security. Generally, when the level of the stock market rises, implied volatility decreases and thus Vega decreases.

Rho: The change in the price of an option contract that results from a change in interest rates. Rho is not an important factor in option pricing in a low interest rate environment. Rho is also not usually an important factor in option pricing in short-term (less than seven months' duration) options.

Volume: The number of shares or contracts traded today.

Open Interest: The number of open or unexercised contracts for each option that are currently outstanding. The number of option contracts outstanding is not like common shares of stock outstanding, because this number is constantly changing according to the specialists' books. Open interest is the best measure of an option's liquidity. Do not trade option contracts that have only a few contracts in open interest. If it is only you and the market maker trading, who do you think will win? It is best to deal in option contracts that have at least five hundred to one thousand contracts in open interest.

Options pricing

Although stock options have been around since the 1880s, they were not actively traded until after 1973. This is when the **Black-Scholes formula** was created to determine the correct price of options. This formula tells us what theoretical price a person should pay for an option. It uses five ingredients to determine what is known as the fair, or theoretical, value that one should pay.

> **Black-Scholes Formula:** A Nobel-Prize-winning pricing model that is used by options exchanges to price options. It considers such factors as the price of the underlying security, option strike price, time remaining until expiration, implied volatility, and the current level of interest rates.

1. The current stock price
2. The strike price you want to trade
3. The time until the expiration of the contract
4. The cost of money (interest rates)
5. The stock's volatility (pricing is based on expected future or implied volatility)

Every option has two parts that make up its value:

1. Intrinsic (or actual market) value
2. Extrinsic (or time) value

If a stock is priced at twenty-six dollars and you would like to buy the stock at the twenty-five-dollar strike price, then you will pay a *minimum* of one dollar for the option. That is the intrinsic value of the option, or its value if it expires right now. In other words, this is the amount necessary for a breakeven trade, if the option expires today.

Depending on a number of factors, you will also pay an amount in excess of the intrinsic value for the option. This is the extrinsic value of the option, and it is calculated based primarily on two things:

1. The amount of time left prior to expiration
2. The volatility of the underlying stock or index

Volatility is a measurement of the *magnitude* of a stock's movement. It does not consider the *direction* in which a stock might move.

The price of an option is made up of intrinsic value plus extrinsic value.

> **LEAPS:** This term refers to Long-term Equity Appreciation Participation Securities. These are options with expiration dates at least six months, and not longer than three years, in the future.

LEAPS are long-term equity appreciation participation securities. They are options that expire in January at least six months, but less than three years, in the future.

In the case of long-term options (**LEAPS**), interest rates can also be a factor in option pricing; however, interest rates are not a significant factor in determining most option prices. Interest rates have almost no effect on options that expire within the next several months. LEAPS are long-term equity appreciation participation securities.

They are options that expire in January at least six months, but less than three years, in the future.

Option Profits—step-by-step rules

1. Option buyers are often speculating and therefore usually lose money in the long run.
2. It is best to be a long-term net buyer of options *only* when you are using them as portfolio insurance. In this case, as in the case of your home insurance, you hope to *lose* your investment.
3. Options are priced by the market makers—in favor of the market makers. They make a living by being net sellers of options to the public.
4. *Sell net premium in order to put the odds in your favor. This strategy can be implemented with a goal of enabling you to achieve a monthly income.*

   > **Sell net premium in order to put the odds in your favor. This strategy can be implemented with a goal of enabling you to achieve a monthly income.**

5. Always use strict rules of entry, risk, and exit. Write your rules down before you enter each trade.
6. Never change your rules during a trade.

CHAPTER 9

Decreasing Your Risk

One definition of an economist is somebody who sees something happen in practice and wonders if it will work in theory.
—**Ronald Reagan**

We are now ready to go into the beginning of a specific strategy that can make you wealthy if you will only follow it with discipline.

Prior to studying this chapter, go back and review chapter 3, "The Miracle of Compound Interest." I have read that Warren Buffet, whom many refer to as the greatest investor of all time, has referred to compound interest as the greatest miracle in the world. Always keep this in mind when planning your investment strategy. You should strive to always keep your wealth growing by consistent small amounts while avoiding setbacks that can destroy the timing and therefore the results of your plan.

Anyone can compute compound interest, but have you ever taken the time to really think about the concept of compounding and relate it to you and your own financial situation? If you can earn compound interest on your money at the rate of 3 percent per month, then you can turn a mere $25,000 account into approximately $1,000,000 in a period of only ten years. This $1,000,000 will then become $40,000,000 in another ten years.

You only need to maintain focus and discipline. Do not let a short run of successful trades make you overconfident and cause you to begin taking risks that are not a part of your game plan. Also, don't get discouraged if a bad month sets you back a bit. Investing is a marathon, not a sprint.

The simplest and least risky method to achieve a monthly income from your portfolio is to sell covered calls against the stocks that are already the long-term holdings of your portfolio. This is a strategy that is employed by many professional traders and investors. As I mentioned previously in this book, Warren Buffet's Berkshire Hathaway Company employs this strategy with many of the stocks that it holds. Berkshire's long-term holdings of stocks such as Coca-Cola, American Express, and other companies have appreciated in value far more than these stocks have gone up in value themselves. Why? Because Buffet often sells covered calls in order to increase the yield on his portfolio. You will notice that he never talks much about his strategies, because he wants to keep them private. If everyone knew what Buffet was doing, then it would make it difficult for him to establish positions, and his strategies might no longer work as well as they have in the past. If you learn to use charting and technical analysis properly, then you can sometimes discover a stock that Buffet is buying prior to his announcing it to the public.

Of course you and I, as retail investors, can move into or out of a position in a few minutes' time. This actually gives us an advantage over the larger and better informed professional investors and hedge funds.

Some people have either a sentimental or a tax reason for not wanting to sell a particular stock. In 2008, a person that I know well watched his Bank of America stock go from forty-five dollars to three dollars per share. This one holding had actually made him wealthy over a number of years, and he could not convince himself to sell it. You should never let this happen to you, because you should always have sell stops in place slightly below the next level of support! If you do this, then you will be stopped out of a declining position before it can hurt your portfolio too much. If this man had sold covered calls against his position and adjusted them every time the short option had lost most of its value, then his loss would have been greatly reduced.

If you own stocks that offer options, then you have the ability to generate a monthly income from those stocks by applying the simple covered call strategy. Selling covered calls is a powerful income-producing strategy that can generate immediate and consistent cash flow.

Many people don't already have a large, diversified portfolio. Therefore, the strategy taught in this book will be to go through a stock selection process each month and assume that every month is a new beginning with another new income goal in mind.

In the real estate example that I used earlier in this book, the owner of the property generated an immediate income of ten thousand dollars by selling an option. Basically, he sold a call option that allowed someone to "call his property away" anytime during the term of the contract. Since he owned the property, he was "covered," enabling him to deliver the property no matter what happened to the value of the property during the time period. In effect, this property owner sold a "covered call" on his real estate holding. He generated income and thereby reduced his risk of ownership. If the property had been rented prior to a transfer, he would have kept this rental income also. This is the equivalent of the fact that you will keep all dividends that a company pays out, even though you may have sold a call that has not yet been exercised.

The covered call strategy

You can use this same approach in the stock market to generate income on stocks that you own. You can sell a right to purchase your stock for a specific amount of time. If the stock price rises above that strike price (as you hope it will), then you will be "called out" of your position. If it does not rise up to that level, then you will keep the option money and sell another option next month. If the stock paid a dividend during this option period, then you will keep this dividend income also.

If, instead, the stock declines considerably below the strike price during the time period, then you should buy the sold option back at profit and sell another call option with a lower strike and the same expiration date. Thus, you can double up on your income and therefore cut your losses considerably on a stock that is falling in price.

If you sell a call with a slightly **OTM** strike price, and the stock appreciates in value, you will be "called out" of your stock. This means that you will automatically sell it at the strike price of the sold call and keep the option money *plus* the profit from the sale. This is a nice experience to have.

> **Out of The Money (OTM):** A call option is OTM when its strike price is above the price of the underlying security. A put option is OTM when its strike price is below the price of the underlying security. If an option is OTM at expiration, then it has no value.

Lower your risk and increase your income

The foundation principal of the covered call strategy is that you must own the underlying stock. If you sell someone else the right to buy a stock that you don't already own, then you have unlimited risk. This is called selling a **naked call** option. It is a very high-risk strategy. Most stockbrokers will allow only the most experienced and well capitalized investors to sell naked options.

> **Naked Call:** A sold, or short, call position that is not supported by any underlying security or hedge position. The maximum risk of a naked call is unlimited. Many brokerages do not permit naked short options except for the most experienced and well capitalized investors.

Selling a covered call is one of the most conservative option trading strategies. It is so conservative that most brokers allow it even in retirement accounts. But it is a very powerful income strategy that most investors do not understand. Unlike in real estate, you do not have to find someone to whom to sell the option. The market will do this for you, usually in a matter of only a few seconds. You need only to place the order.

One option contract controls one hundred shares of stock. You should sell one option contract for each one hundred shares of stock that you own. Since you own the stock, you are "covered" from suffering an unlimited loss in the event of a rapid price increase. No matter how high the price of the stock goes, you can meet your obligation.

Assessing the risks

In selling a covered call:

1. You actually have less risk of loss than in owning a stock. This is because, if the stock goes down, then you at least have decreased your cost basis by selling the call. If the stock continues to decline in price, then the sold option will have a market value that declines considerably. You can take advantage of this and double your income by buying back the sold option at a profit and selling another option that expires in the same month but at a lower strike price than the strike price of the first sold option. This second sale is an additional credit to your account, and it further decreases your losses in a declining market. If you sell one or more calls against your position every month, then you continue to decrease your cost basis, and therefore you decrease your risk every month for as long as you own the stock.

2. You have given up the *opportunity cost* of profiting big in the event of a rapid rise in the price of the stock.

You have, in effect, put a "ceiling" on your profits. The maximum gain is the profit from selling your stock at the strike price plus the premium of the option. At first, this may not sound like such a good strategy, unless you have adapted your mind-set to adhering to the goal that we set at the beginning of this book of achieving a consistent gain of 3–5 percent per month.

If you think about it, few stocks have ever appreciated thirty-six percent per year, year after year, over an extended period of time. If you ever hit on the unusual circumstance of owning one of these winners, you can be wealthy over a period of time. But you can easily and consistently sell covered calls on a number of safe stocks in major companies and achieve this same return on investment every month, time and time again. If you do this, you are putting the odds of winning in your favor.

You can shift the risk and put the odds in your favor

When asked the question "Which way do stocks move?" most people respond by saying, "They either move up or down."

This is not true! They can move up, down, or stay approximately the same. In fact, most of the time stocks move in a sideways channel.

We want to play an odds game in the stock market. Selling covered calls can shift these odds in your favor. In chapter 2, a comparison was made between the stock market and a casino. Decide for yourself that you are a player that will set the odds in your favor and therefore play to win!

CHAPTER 10

Instant Income through Selling Covered Calls

> Every failure will teach you a lesson that you need to learn, if only you will keep your eyes and ears open and be willing to be taught. Every adversity is usually a blessing in disguise.
> —**Napoleon Hill**

We are now ready to go over the specific rules that one must follow in order to place a covered call trade. This involves first buying a stock, index, or ETF which will act as the underlying or base security against which you will generate an income stream.

Rules of the stock selection process

1. Select a stock, index, or ETF to purchase.

You should maintain a watch list of stocks that you review at least weekly. Add to and subtract from this list as conditions with the specific company, the stock market, and the economy change.

Stock selection for selling covered calls is different from stock selection for buy-and-hold investing for appreciation. It is important that you select stocks that you would not mind holding as long-term investments. However, the expectation of short- to intermediate-term price appreciation is not the most important characteristic for which to search. You mainly want stocks that do not go down, because you are relying on a strategy of making your income by selling calls against them. Large, well known, and stable companies that you have heard about all of your life are the first place to look. Remember that your goal is to make a consistent income of 3–5 percent per month.

Do not simply choose stocks that have the highest priced calls. These calls are high priced for a reason, even though the reason may not be known to the general public. This strategy can lead to losses in the underlying stock that are greater than the income from selling the call.

Sources for screening stocks
a. The first source that you should use is your general knowledge of large, stable companies that you have known about all of your life or that you continually hear about on television or read about in the newspapers. Some of these include the following: MCD, JNJ, WMT, IBM, GIS, BAX, MMM, DD, HPQ, HON, KO, PM, MO, MON, T, YUM, PEP, PG, POT, PM, CAT, DE, BNI, FCX, XOM, COP, K, KFT, HNZ, etc.

Again, do not choose stocks upon which to sell covered calls only because they have very high premiums. If the call makes you 6 percent, but the stock declines 20 percent during the month, then you have defeated the purpose of the transaction.

   b. The second source of stocks to screen should come from the newspaper *Investor's Business Daily*. This is an excellent newspaper that I recommend to any serious investor. There are several valuable sections that appear in it once a week. These include IBD Top 100 Stocks, IBD 200 Worst Fundamentals, and IBD 200 Best Fundamentals. IBD also ranks every listed stock every day, based on its fundamental and technical outlook. You can make a mental note of the stocks that IBD calls to your attention each week and decide upon ones to add to your watch list.

1. As your third source of locating stocks, you should subscribe to at least one publication that recommends fundamentally strong stocks to long-term investors. You do not need to purchase the very expensive stock newsletters. One that I recommend is *Personal Finance,* Elliott H. Gue, Editor. You can easily find others online. I do not recommend paying more than approximately one hundred dollars per year for a newsletter.

From these basic sources, you should establish and maintain a watch list, to which you should always be adding and subtracting stock candidates. Each month, when it is time to create your income trades, go to this watch list and buy a diversified cross section of stocks against which to sell calls. A portfolio of ten to fifteen stocks is recommended. Do not get so many that you have a difficult time following your positions. You might start out with only two or three and build up from there over time.

Use technical analysis to time purchases and sells
From the stocks on your watch list, buy only stocks that meet the rules that we set out earlier with regard to the following.

- Trend line: Only buy stocks that are in an uptrend.
- Support: The stock should be at either trend line or horizontal support.
- MACD: The direction of the *weekly* MACD Histogram should be *up*. The daily MACD Histogram should ideally be below zero and rising.
- Stochastic: The stochastic measurement should ideally be in the oversold position and rising. If it is not, it should at least be rising. Do not buy if the daily stochastic is in the overbought position or if it is falling.
- Elder-Ray: Preferably the bull and bear lines are both negative and rising. Do not buy if both are in positive territory.
- Bollinger Bands: It is usually best to buy when the price is near the bottom of the Bollinger Band channel, or at least bouncing off of a moving average line in the middle of the band.

2. Select the option to sell.

Depending on the option pricing table, you will usually want to choose to sell the call option that has the highest *extrinsic* value. This will usually be the option with a strike price closest to the current stock price. If you are extremely positive on a stock, and the option prices are high, then you may want to choose one strike price higher. This will permit you to maximize the overall return (premium plus appreciation) for that particular month.

On the other hand, if you want to have minimum risk together with possibly a lower monthly cash yield, then you may want to sell an option that is slightly in-the-money (ITM) and expect to get called out. Depending on the level of the volatility index ($VIX), this low-risk strategy can often yield a very safe and stable income of 2–3 percent per month. When the $VIX is high, the general level of option prices is high, and when the $VIX is low, this general level of option prices is low.

3. Calculate the expected return on investment.

Calculate three possible returns for the next month. First, calculate the return if the stock price remains unchanged. Second, calculate the return if the stock goes

> **Always establish a stop loss sell point. It is usually best to place a stop loss order immediately after you complete the purchase of the stock.**

up and therefore gets called away from you. Third, calculate the return in the event that the stock declines in value to your stop loss point and you get stopped out. This is your maximum loss.

Always establish a stop loss sell point. It is usually best to place a stop loss order immediately after you complete the purchase of the stock.

4. Calculate the correct number of shares of stock to buy based on the maximum risk formula that we will cover in the money management section later in this book.
5. Buy the stock and sell the call option.
6. Monitor the position.

The primary adjustment to this simple position occurs in the event the stock goes down. Then you can either let a sell stop activate or double up on your income by buying back the short option at a profit and selling a new position option (in the same month) that is one or more strikes lower than the previous position. This second alternative is usually the best one in a well known, safe company with good fundamentals, especially if the price of the stock has not broken its trend line.

7. Close out the trade.

This is done by either letting the option expire worthless, or by buying it back during the expiration week. If the above selection items remain positive for ownership of the position, then sell a call against it again in the next month.

A covered call example

1. Select the stock to purchase.

Let's say that on April 9, 2010, we decide to analyze a position to buy stock and sell a covered call on Potash

Corp. See Exhibit 10 (a weekly chart) and Exhibit 11 (a daily chart).

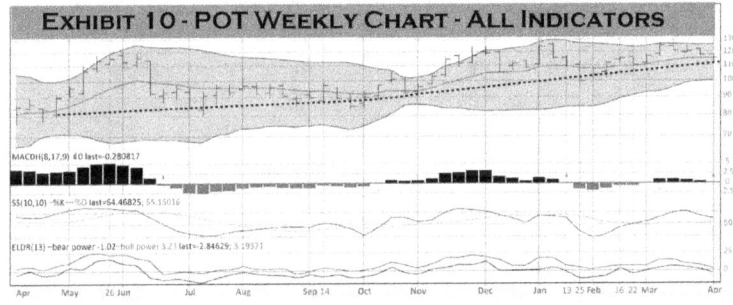

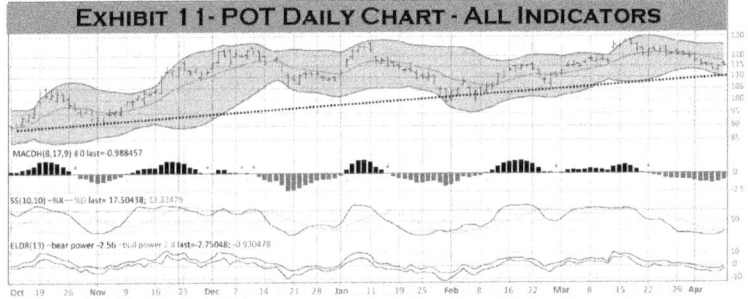

Technical indicators

a. Trend line: The trend line is the dashed line on the charts. On these Exhibits, we can see that *the trend of the stock is up* on both the weekly and the daily charts. This is necessary in order to approve a buy.

b. Support: The trend line is acting as the support line on both the daily and the weekly charts. On both charts, the current price is close enough to this support trend line to justify a purchase at this time.

c. MACD Histogram: The direction of the *weekly* MACD histogram is down. This means that we should not buy this stock at this point. The direction of the daily MACD Histogram is below zero and just beginning to rise. This daily condition is a positive one that indicates good timing for a purchase.

d. Stochastic: This indicator (which is indicated by SS under the price chart) should be viewed on the daily charts only, because it is a timing indicator. This indicator is oversold and rising. This is a signal that it is okay to buy.

e. Elder-Ray: On the daily charts, both the bull line and the bear line are below zero and rising. This is an ideal situation. Only view the daily charts for Elder-Ray decisions, because it is a timing indicator only.

f. Bollinger Bands: On the daily chart, the price is below the middle of the channel range. This is a positive sign. We view Bollinger Bands on the daily chart only, because it is a timing indicator.

This stock is showing buy signals on every indicator except for the negative slope of the weekly MACD Histogram. Therefore, we should follow our buy/sell rules and wait for this MACD Histogram to turn positive prior to a purchase of this stock. The positive indications of all five other technical signals indicate that this stock should be followed closely. It is probable that a buying opportunity will come soon. You will rarely ever find a stock in which *all* factors point to a buy. While many experienced traders might wait to purchase this stock, we will use it as an example.

On April 9, 2010, Potash closed at $115.19, which was up $.62 on the day.

1. We will assume a purchase of the stock for $115.19 per share.
2. Select the option to sell.

Exhibit 12 is an April 9 options table for Potash for the month of May, 2010.

Exhibit 12

9-Apr-10

Options Table

POT   Price: $115.19   40 Days to expiration

May 2010 - Expiration

Calls		Strike Price	Puts	
Bid	**Ask**		**Bid**	**Ask**
16	**16.2**	100	1	1.05
12	**12.15**	105	1.97	2.02
8.55	**8.7**	110	3.5	3.6
5.85	6	115	5.8	5.9
3.85	3.95	120	**8.75**	**8.9**
2.44	2.53	125	**12.35**	**12.5**
1.52	1.58	130	**16.4**	**16.55**
0.93	0.98	135	**20.8**	**20.95**

Prices in bold face type are In The Money and therefore have intrinsic value.

Prices in regular type have only time value as of this date.

Assumptions:

a. If we expect the price to continue rising, we could enter a limit order to sell the May $120 call option. This gives the buyer the right to call away our stock for a price equal to $120 per share, which will be a profit to us of $120-$115.19 = $4.81 in addition to the call premium, which we will keep. The price or premium for which we will sell the call option is the halfway point between the bid and ask prices (this halfway point is called the mark), or, in this example, $3.90. You should sell one option contract for every one hundred shares of stock that you buy. These options expire on May 21, 2010, which is forty days from today.

b. If we want to reduce the **break-even** point and thus lower our risk, we could instead sell the May $115 call option. This allows the buyer of the call

> **Break-even:** The price (usually at the expiration of an option) at which the transaction neither makes nor loses money.

to buy or call away our POT stock for a price equal to $115 per share, which is a loss to us equal to $.19 per share. However, in exchange for selling this call option, we receive an amount equal to $5.92 per share. This second alternative raises the monthly yield, if the price remains unchanged, but it lowers the called out yield in the event the stock continues to increase in price. Many covered call sellers automatically sell the call with the *highest extrinsic value*.

In this case, it's the $115 call for a price equal to $5.92 per share.

3. Calculate the possible returns on investment. On the $120 call, these are as follows:

   a. Return if stock price remains unchanged: $3.90/115.19 = 3.4 percent.

   b. Return if stock is called out: $3.90+ 4.81/115.19 =7.6 percent.

   c. Break-even -point: $115.19-3.90 = $111.29

As long as the stock remains above $111.29 on May 21, you are making money on this transaction. In other words, if the price of the underlying stock decreases by 3.4 percent or less, then you are still making money.

4. Calculate the amount of stock to buy.

   a. You can see in Exhibit 11 that support for POT is at about $110 per share (the dashed line). If the stock closes below this price, then the trend line would be broken. If this trend line is broken, then one must assume that the uptrend might be finished and a sale of the stock would be in order.

   b. A protective stop loss order should be placed 3 percent below this support base or at $110 x .97 = $106.70. Do not place the stop loss order exactly at the price support level, because you need to give the stock a bit of room to fluctuate. In this example, we need to give the $110 support line some room for error, rather than place our stop at exactly at $110.

Thus, we will place a contingent order to automatically sell the underlying stock and repurchase the option, if the price falls below $106.70.

c. The risk in this transaction is therefore $115.19-$106.70 = $8.49 per share *less* the amount for which we sold the covered call, or $3.90. This is $8.49-$3.90 = $4.59 per share.

d. The reason that we subtracted the entire price of the unexpired sold option from the loss incurred, even though this option is not yet expired, is this: if the price of the stock has fallen all the way to $106.70, then we can assume that we can buy this option back for very close to zero.

e. Set the maximum risk at an amount not to exceed 2 percent of the total account value. Thus, if an account value is equal to $100,000, then the maximum risk per transaction should not exceed $2,000.

f. Divide the risk per share of $4.59 by the maximum loss of $2,000, and you get the number of shares that can be bought without violating the excess risk in any one security rule. Therefore, in a $100,000 account, you can buy a *maximum* of 435 shares of stock, which you will round down to 400 shares. You must buy the stock in increments of 100 shares, because that is the number of shares in one option contract. At a purchase price of $115.19 x 400 = $46,076 worth of stock. However, rule *g* below will supersede this maximum risk rule and require that we make a downward adjustment to the number of shares. This is because placing 46 percent of an account into one stock is too much concentration of risk.

g. Also we must consider the percentage of total portfolio value that can be invested into any one position; it is wise to set a limit of no more than 15 percent in any one issue. Fifteen percent of $100,000 is $15,000. This $15,000 divided by $115.19 per share is equal to 130 shares. Because shares must be purchased in round lots of 100 in order to match them up with option contracts sold, this means you can purchase 100 shares. If you are close to the next 100 share purchase, you should go ahead and round up, because this will take into consideration the credit that you will receive for the sold options.

h. Never allow the total maximum risk of all issues in the entire portfolio added together to exceed 10 percent of the account value. If you chose to also play the downside by selling short the stock of companies that you believe will decrease in value and creating income by selling put contracts against these positions, then you can allow your risk to approach 10 percent on *each side* of the market. In this way, you are creating your own hedge fund without paying the unreasonable fees charged by hedge fund managers. Hedge fund managers have a standard fee equal to 2 percent of the asset value per annum, plus 20 percent of the profit. Always keep some cash in reserve in order to take advantage of new opportunities and to play another day in case of a catastrophe.

5. Buy the stock and sell the calls.

In the example above, buy 100 shares of stock and sell one call option contract at the chosen strike price. In this example, you could buy 100 shares of stock at a $115.20 limit order or an amount of $11,520. You would then also sell one May $120 call contract at a price of $3.90 or 100 x $3.90 = $390. See exhibit 12. This $390 would immediately be deposited into your account, and your out-of-pocket investment is equal to $115.20-$3.90 = $111.30 x 100 = $11,130.

6. Monitor the position.

If the stock stays the same throughout the entire month, you can let the current month option expire, and then sell the next month option for another income stream. If the stock goes up, I usually prefer to let it get called out and then take my money and go on to another trade. If the stock goes down, but not to the stop loss point, you should buy back the sold option at a profit and then sell the next lower strike price option in order to double up on your monthly income. If you can buy back a short option for a price that reflects a decrease of 75 percent of the extrinsic value that was sold, this is usually a good decision. This second sale can offset any losses on the underlying stock. However, if the stock goes to the stop loss point, then sell it, take your profit on the option by buying it back, and exit the position.

7. Close out the trade

Monitor the trade closely during expiration week. If the option price of the sold call becomes very low, it may be wise to cut your risk by buying it back prior to expiration and selling the next month's call option at a higher price that reflects the longer period of time to expiration.

At this point in our live seminars, we go over various examples of live covered call trades so that everyone can understand exactly how to enter into and manage these trades. A seminar schedule can be found at: www.incomestrategiesacademy.com.

CHAPTER 11

LEAPS: Achieve Huge Profits by Employing Financial Leverage

> The only thing that hurts more than paying an income tax is not having income to pay an income tax on.
> —**Harvey Friedentag**

Be Like Lance!

The first stock and options seminar that I ever attended was taught by a man we shall call Lance. He was an investor who had apparently done quite well for his own account. He had a beautiful wife and a mansion on the intercoastal waterway in South Florida complete with a yacht in back, tennis courts, spa, and private pool. He was driving a $200,000 sports car that goes faster than I ever want to go. I was fortunate that the seminar was in my hometown, but most people had traveled a great distance in order to get there. At the end of the seminar, people were leaving quickly in order to get to the airport or to get on the road for a long drive home.

> **You will never get wealthy trading time for money!**

I noticed that Lance and his wife were in no hurry, so I asked them to join me at my favorite restaurant for a glass of wine and some appetizers on me. We had a great discussion wherein I realized that I was crazy if I ever went back to any day-to-day workplace or job other than investing. You will never get wealthy trading time for money!

Lance is a dentist who was working long hours in order to support a good lifestyle for his family. He noticed a neighbor who seemed never to work but who always had more money than anyone else in the neighborhood. Finally, Lance asked him, "How do you do it?"

Well, to make a long story short, the result of that conversation was that Lance left the practice of dentistry within one year and has never looked back. Lance learned how to sell covered calls and later how to pyramid his profits by using LEAPS as his underlying security (or cover). He is making much more money than he ever did as a dentist. More importantly, he now has time to travel and to do things with his family that he had never been able to do before.

The important end to this story is that I asked Lance, "Why do you spend your valuable time conducting these seminars teaching people how to do what you do?"

I was taken aback by his answer, and I have made it a point to try to live up to his high standards. He said, "Well, someone along the way took their valuable time to teach me how to do this and thereby to achieve more success than I had ever dreamed possible. They charged me very little for it. In fact, I paid myself back the cost of their seminar in only three months and after that, it's been all profit. I owe it back to society to do the same and help others. I am going to do this teaching and coaching for a short period of time, maybe several more years, and then my debt will be repaid."

Like Lance, I want to give back to others. I am writing this book, and I teach seminars from time to time, in order to repay my debt to mankind which was received from various mentors who took the time to teach me how to achieve more success than I had ever dreamed possible.

Financial leverage

Investors that desire to increase their return on investment through the use of financial **leverage** have traditionally done so by opening a margin account with a brokerage firm and borrowing money against their stock holdings in order to buy additional stock and thereby pyramid their profits. Under Regulation T, the SEC allows brokerage firms to lend you money for this purpose with a restriction that the maximum loan amount is 50 percent of the initial purchase price of the stock, with a maintenance requirement of 30 percent of the original purchase price. This means that if the price of your security decreases to the point that your equity value divided by the

> **Leverage:** In finance, leverage refers to the use of debt to supplement an investment. This use will generally substantially increase or decrease the percentage return on investment.

total value of the position is less than 30 percent, you must either put up additional money or close the position by paying off the loan and selling your stock. Brokerage firms hold common stock and other liquid financial instruments as security for these loans and charge interest at a rate that is usually quite high given the low risk and high liquidity of the loan. Of course, this interest expense that the brokerage deducts from your account every month eats into your profit as time passes.

In the last two chapters of this book, I will discuss how to use LEAPS and synthetic stock positions in order to get financial leverage at a much lower cost than borrowing on margin. This leverage, or extra buying power, can possibly catapult your returns far beyond the 3–5 percent per month that we have previously discussed.

It is important that you do not try to use these leveraged position methods until you have first completely mastered the tactics that have been previously set forth in this book.

LEAPS defined

LEAPS refer to Long-term Equity Appreciation Participation Securities. In 1991, the CBOE introduced LEAPS, or long-term options on stocks and indexes. These options offer expiration dates up to two and a half years into the future. They can be used as a low-cost substitute for owning shares of stock in a covered call program. LEAPS are available on hundreds of stocks and on most indexes.

If you compare the cost versus the benefit of owning borrowed securities to owning LEAPS, you will often find that you can achieve several significant benefits with LEAPS. These are:

- There is less risk in owning LEAPS than in borrowing to purchase more stock. If the stock goes down in price, you must still pay back the entire loan amount plus interest; yet you will derive much less money from the sales proceeds than you originally paid for the stock. Whereas, with the LEAPS, the price of the option contract is the total risk, and it should be considerably less than the price for which the stock sells.
- The price of the LEAPS can often be purchased at a discount to the rate of interest that would be paid, if the funds were borrowed in order to purchase additional stock. In other words, the LEAPS extrinsic value (that will evaporate with time) is less than the amount of interest expense that would be incurred if the extra shares were purchased with borrowed funds.

LEAPS work just like any other stock option. The contracts are based on one hundred shares of stock, and they have a specific strike price and a specific expiration date. There are LEAPS calls and LEAPS puts. LEAPS have the following unique characteristics:

- They only have January expiration dates. Some stocks have LEAPS for the next two years out in time. This January expiration must be at least seven months into the future. After this date (June of each year), the options still exist, but they are no longer referred to as LEAPS.
- LEAPS have a different symbol root than the other options on the same stock.

One should approach buying LEAPS calls the same as they would buying a stock. In other words, you want the underlying stock to be in an uptrend and at a buy point. Do not buy LEAPS calls unless you would consider the underlying stock to be a purchase candidate. Do not buy LEAPS puts unless you would consider selling short the underlying stock.

In this book, we will limit our discussion of LEAPS to their use as a stock substitute in selling covered calls. Keep in mind that there are other uses for LEAPS, such as for portfolio insurance.

LEAPS—the risk factors

1. LEAPS are options, and in buying them, you can lose 100 percent of your investment, even though the underlying stock still has value.

2. *When buying LEAPS, you should always use a sell stop that is based on the price support of the underlying stock.* Do not use a sell stop that is based on the price of the LEAPS itself. If you do, the options market makers may take you out of the position even though the underlying stock price never justified this trade.

3. Although LEAPS will incur smaller dollar value movement than the underlying security, the *percentage* move will be larger with LEAPS. Therefore, you must set your stop loss carefully and manage your 2 percent maximum loss cautiously.

Success with LEAPS—the reasons

Remember that the price of an option is made up of its intrinsic (or real) value plus the extrinsic (or time) value. *Options do not lose the extrinsic*

> **Options do not lose the extrinsic value portion of their price in a linear relationship to the passing of time.**

value portion of their price in a linear relationship to the passing of time. Extrinsic value evaporates much more quickly as the option approaches its expiration date. Because LEAPS have a long period of time until expiration, they lose the extrinsic value portion of their price much more slowly than do short-term options. Likewise, short-term options lose their extrinsic value much more quickly than do options expiring in the distant future. This is the reason for buying a long-term in-the-money (ITM) call option with a high delta and selling an at-the-money (ATM) short-term call option with a delta approximately equal to fifty. A good options table should provide the delta of each option contract.

- If the price of the underlying security stays the same or even moves down a little, you should have a profitable trade, because you have sold time value that evaporates more rapidly than the time value that you purchased. In this case, you can just sit back and wait to collect your money.

- If the price of the underlying security moves up, you are covered for your possible losses in the sold call option by the even greater appreciation in the price of the LEAPS. This is because the delta of the LEAPS is much higher than the delta of the sold call. In this case, you will have a profit that is even greater than your profit in the unchanged underlying security example above.

- If there is a large downward move in the price of the underlying security, you need to automatically limit your losses. You do this by always having a sell stop in place as the ultimate protection. You should also roll down your current month short call position whenever it can be bought back cheaply. By "roll down," I mean buy it back at a profit and sell another call in the same month with a lower strike price. "Cheaply" means for 75 percent or less of extrinsic value that you sold.

Use LEAPS to increase your buying power

LEAPS offer leverage for a long-term position. They offer an opportunity to benefit from the leverage of margin investing without having to pay margin interest. Of course, LEAPS have some extrinsic value, which results in incurring some loss in value due to time decay. Common stock positions do not have this loss in value due to time decay. However, the value lost due to time decay can be minimized, if the correct LEAPS are chosen. The higher the delta of the LEAPS, the less the time or extrinsic value.

By using LEAPS, one can control a larger block of stock with less capital than it costs to buy the same number of shares of actual stock. *This allows you to sell more same-month calls and therefore earn more monthly income.*

The higher the delta of the LEAPS, the more closely the price movement of the LEAPS will mirror the price movement of the underlying stock. The relationship between the price movement of a stock and its option contracts is referred to

> **The higher the delta of the LEAPS, the more closely the price movement of the LEAPS will mirror the price movement of the underlying stock.**

as the delta (the Greek symbol). The delta tells us how much an option goes up or down when the stock goes up or down by one dollar. The more intrinsic value an option has, the higher the delta will be. If this intrinsic value is close to the total price of an option, then the option's price movement will be close to a one-to-one relationship with the stock. This would result in a delta of 1.00 (the same profit or loss as owning the stock, but at a lower cost basis). One can often find options with a delta close to 1.00, but with a price far lower than the price of the stock. Thus, we would have a pure stock substitute (exactly the same as owning the stock) but for a much lower cost. The result is that you will have a position with positive leverage but with no interest or carrying charges (since you did not borrow any money) and often very little extrinsic value which will result in loss due to time decay. If you borrow to acquire additional stock, then you will have interest expenses. If instead you own the LEAPS, there is no interest expense. There is only extrinsic value evaporation.

Note that the delta of a LEAPS will change with time and with price movement. Therefore, you must constantly monitor the delta of the LEAPS and compare it to the delta of the sold current month option. You never want the delta of the sold front-month option to be greater than the delta of the option that you purchased.

This will result in negative theta and thus a loss with the passing of time.

When selling calls against a LEAPS position, it is recommended to look for a LEAPS with a delta between .70 and .90. This will usually obtain a good leverage ratio (low price relative to the stock) while allowing for a reasonably close to mirror movement between the LEAPS and the underlying stock. Note that LEAPS do not rise or fall in value dollar for dollar when a stock goes up or down. It moves in relation to its delta. Some might argue that the risk is therefore less than owning stock. However, keep in mind that the percentage change in the price of the LEAPS in this example is *greater* than the percentage change in the price of the stock.

Steps to using LEAPS as a stock substitute:

1. Analyze the underlying stock as described previously. Do *not* buy LEAPS unless you would also want to buy the stock.

2. Observe the open interest. Do *not* buy LEAPS if there is not sufficient open interest or liquidity so that you feel that you can sell it on a reasonable basis. If it's only you and the market maker playing the game when you want to sell, then it will most likely be a bad experience for you. I would be very cautious about owning LEAPS that have less than five hundred contracts in open interest outstanding.

3. Observe the delta of the LEAPS. It is usually best to buy LEAPS with a delta ranging from .70–.90. Keep a watch on the delta throughout the trade. It will

change with the price of the underlying security and with the passing of time.

4. Choose the LEAPS call to be bought. Compare the premium at various levels of delta. If there is too much of a premium at all levels, do not buy the LEAPS; buy the stock. Always compare the price premium of the LEAPS to buying the stock on 50 percent margin and paying interest.

5. Choose the call to be sold using the same method as you would in selling a covered call. Always sell in the closest month, unless you are in the week of expiration. Even during this last week, you may want to sell the closest month. The last week prior to expiration has a great deal of time decay.

6. Calculate the monthly return on the transaction as if:
   a. The stock does not move
   b. The stock moves to the strike price of the short call
   c. The stock moves down to the sell stop

7. Always put a sell stop on the LEAPS based on the price support level of the underlying security. Make sure that you buy back the short call at a profit, if the sell stop is exercised. Do not let it remain as a naked position. Your broker may make you buy back the short call first. If this is the case, your sell stop may not be automatically exercised. Be sure to check with your broker in order that you know how your account is handled and act accordingly.

Important note: Do not attempt to use the LEAPS-leveraged method of investing until you have successfully learned and mastered how to sell, manage, repurchase, and roll over a simple covered call investment program. Make sure that you practice selling calls against LEAPS many times as a paper trade only before you venture into this strategy with your real money. I do not want you to lose money in the learning process and become discouraged just before you are on the verge of a huge success.

How to calculate yield comparisons when using LEAPS

Example 1: See Exhibits 13 and 14

Exhibit 13

13-Feb-09

Options Table

IBM   Price: $93.84   93.84   336 Days to expiration

January 2010 - Expiration

Calls					Strike Price	Puts				
Delta	Open Interest	Intrinsic	Bid	Ask		Bid	Ask	Delta	Open Interest	Intrinsic
0.87	79	38.84	40.2	41.3	55	2.3	2.45	0.09	1279	0
0.85	286	33.84	36	37	60	3	3.3	0.12	3956	0
0.82	41	28.84	31.9	32.6	65	4	4.3	0.15	3531	0
0.79	862	23.84	28.1	28.5	70	5.2	5.4	0.19	4256	0
0.75	77	18.84	24.4	24.7	75	6.4	6.8	0.23	3135	0
0.7	1621	13.84	21	21.4	80	7.9	8.4	0.28	5914	0
0.65	1090	8.84	17.9	16.2	85	9.7	10.2	0.34	2595	0
0.6	7002	3.84	15	15.3	90	11.8	12.3	0.39	6158	0
0.54	1871	0	12.5	12.7	95	14.1	14.7	0.45	984	1.16
0.48	9131	0	10.1	10.4	100	16.7	17.3	0.52	5959	6.16
0.42	894	0	8.1	8.7	105	19.6	20.4	0.58	155	11.16

Prices in bold face type are In The Money and therefore have intrinsic value.

Prices in regular type have only time value as of this date.

Exhibit 14

13-Feb-09

Options Table

IBM Price: $93.84   35 Days to expiration

March 2009 - Expiration

Calls						Puts				
					Strike Price					
Delta	Open Interest	Intrinsic	Bid	Ask		Bid	Ask	Delta	Open Interest	Intrinsic
0.99	0	38.84	38.6	39.3	55	0	0.1	0.01	279	0
0.97	0	33.84	33.7	34.4	60	0.05	0.15	0.01	455	0
0.95	1	28.84	28.7	29.4	65	0.1	0.2	0.02	858	0
0.93	3	23.84	23.8	24.2	70	0.2	0.3	0.04	1497	0
0.91	108	18.84	19.1	19.4	75	0.4	0.5	0.07	2198	0
0.87	1997	13.84	14.5	14.7	80	0.8	0.85	0.12	5642	0
0.79	1889	8.84	10.2	10.4	85	1.5	1.6	0.21	3298	0
0.65	6550	3.84	6.4	6.6	90	2.7	2.8	0.35	6498	0
0.47	7716	0	3.5	3.6	95	4.7	4.9	0.54	4337	1.16
0.28	10497	0	1.5	1.6	100	7.7	7.9	0.75	2087	6.16
0.13	3868	0	0.5	0.6	105	11.6	11.8	0.95	88	11.16

Prices in bold face type are In The Money and therefore have intrinsic value.

Prices in regular type have only time value as of this date.

Call Sold Against a LEAPS Position
IBM February 13, 2009
Price = $93.84

Buy LEAPS/Sell a front month (March) call

1. Calculate the percentage amount of extrinsic premium to be paid:

Exhibit 13 is a February 13, 2009, options table for the month of January 2010 (LEAPS).

Percentage extrinsic premium = (total premium - intrinsic value) divided by stock price.

January 10 call at 80 strike: 21.20 - 13.84/93.84 = 7.36/93.84 = 7.8 percent

January 10 call at 70 strike: 28.30 - 23.84/93.84 = 4.46/93.84 = 4.8 percent

January 10 call at 60 strike: 36.50 - 33.84/93.84 = 2.66/93.84 = 2.8 percent

2. Observe the deltas:

   80 strike—70

   70 strike—79

   60 strike—85

3. Observe the open interest of each strike price. If there is not enough float or contracts traded, then be cautious using this strike price.

   80 strike—1,621

   70 strike—862

   60 strike—286

   It is usually not wise to own LEAPS with less than five hundred contracts in open interest. You do not want to face a lack of liquidity when it's time to sell. Therefore, be careful of buying the 60 strike in this example.

4. Choose the call to be bought.

   In this example, the conservative choice is the 60 strike, but one must be careful of the open interest liquidity shortfall. The most aggressive choice is the 80 strike. It has a good open interest position (1,621 contracts) and, at a price of $21.20, it costs less than the other choices (resulting in more leverage), but it also has a higher portion of the premium that is extrinsic value. This means that the intrinsic (or real) value is a smaller percentage of the total premium than the other choices.

In the first example, we will use the 60 strike option. Except for its lack of liquidity, it is the conservative choice. Its price is $36.50 and its premium to the current stock price is only 2.8 percent. We cannot borrow money for this interest rate. It is selling at 36.50/93.84 = 39 percent of the price of the stock. Thus your invested dollars are leveraged almost three times instead of two times, as would be the case with a 50 percent loan to value Regulation T margin loan.

5. Choose the call to be sold:

    Exhibit 14 is a February 13, 2009, options table for the month of March (next month out).

    With the current price of IBM at $93.84, we will sell the March 95 call at a premium of $3.50 (the midpoint between the bid and ask prices). Because the price of the stock is below the strike price of this short option, its intrinsic value is zero, and the entire premium is extrinsic value and will go to zero at the expiration date, if the stock price does not rise to at least $95 per share. This call offers some appreciation possibility in the LEAPS. It is also the March call that has the highest extrinsic value (premium minus intrinsic value).

    At the expiration of the short call, the price of the stock will be either above, below, or the same as the price at which it is selling today. Let us examine the monthly yields based upon an example of each possibility.

6. Monthly yield calculation:

   Using the 60 strike LEAPS at a price or premium of $36.50 (This is the midpoint between the bid and the asked prices. You can usually get an order filled at this midpoint, though it may take a short while.)

   a. Monthly yield if not the stock does not move:

   $3.50/$36.50 = 9.5 percent

   b. Monthly yield if stock moves to $95 or above:

   i. Calculate the gain from price movement:

   $95.00 - $93.84 = $1.16

   $1.16 x .85 (delta) = $ .99 Appreciation in the LEAPS

   ii. Calculate the gain from selling the call option:

   $3.50

   iii. Add these two components of gain to get total profit:

   $3.50 (sold premium) + $.99 (appreciation in the LEAPS) = $4.49

   iv. Calculate the monthly percentage gain:

   $4.49/$36.50 = 12.3 percent

   c. Monthly yield if the stock declines in value to $90:

   i. Calculate the loss from price movement:

   $93.84 - $90.00 = $-3.84

   $-3.84 x .85 (delta) = $-3.26

ii. Calculate the gain from selling the call option:

$3.50

iii. Add these two components to get total profit or loss:

$-3.26 + $3.50 = $.24

iv. Calculate the monthly percentage gain:

$.24/$36.50 = .7 percent

In example 1, scenario c, the stock went down from $93.84 to $90 (a 4 percent decline), yet you still made money this month!

Note: Do not let the sold front-month call expire! Instead be sure to buy it back prior to its expiration. The LEAPS is a monetary hedge against a price increase in the underlying stock, but it cannot be used for delivery of the stock, if it is called.

Unless its strike price is comfortably above the current stock price, you *must* buy back the sold front-month option prior to expiration.

> **Option Holder:** The owner of a call or a put option.

If this short option's strike price is even anywhere close to the current stock price, you should buy back the short call. If you don't buy back these short options and the monthly closing price is even one cent above the strike price, then your brokerage firm will buy the stock in your account (charging a commission and also perhaps a penalty to your account) and then assign it to the **option holder** at the strike price. The LEAPS cannot be substituted for stock. You will still own the LEAPS.

You may question why someone would exercise an option and then sell the stock in order to make one cent. This is an amount that is less than the commission of the transaction. The answer to this is that you are playing against market makers who deal in many thousands of options and who pay no commissions. Computer generated programs perform these settlement transactions automatically.

After you buy back the sold option, you should then sell the next month's call option in order to generate next month's income.

It is important to recognize that these calculations do not take into consideration the fact that there will be some price decrease on the LEAPS that is due to time decay. This will result in a decrease in the yield by a small amount, but this decrease will be minimal if the LEAPS are far out in time and have a high delta.

Example 1 calculated three monthly yields comparing selling a call against a LEAPS on IBM stock as of February 13, 2009, based upon buying the January of 2010 60 strike at $36.50, and selling a call on the March 95 strike at $3.50. Now let's look at a different LEAPS in the same month.

Example 2: *(See Exhibits 13 and 14)*

In the next example, we will go through another calculation that is based upon choosing to purchase a different and more aggressive LEAPS—the January of 2010, 80 strike.

Buy: January 2010, 80 strike

Price = $21.20—Note that is the midpoint between the bid and asked prices.

Intrinsic value = $13.84

Extrinsic premium paid: ($21.20-$13.84)/93.84 = $7.36/$93.84 = 7.8 percent

Note that there are eleven months remaining until this option expires; therefore the monthly cost or extrinsic evaporation of time value is 7.8/11= .71 percent per month, or 8.52 percent per annum.

Remember, however, that the time or extrinsic value of options does not decay or evaporate on a straight line basis. Most of this extrinsic cost to you on the long option will come during the last six months of the life of this option. LEAPS are options with seven to thirty-one months' life remaining. Therefore, when it gets to the seventh month prior to expiration (June), you should sell it and roll into the option that is nineteen months out in time.

This extrinsic value evaporation (or cost of holding the contract) is lower than most broker margin rates of interest. Compare this to the monthly extrinsic evaporation on the front-month sold call, which is $3.50. In this example, 3.50/21.20 (the cost of the LEAPS) = 16.5 percent per month.

Open interest = 1,621 contracts
Delta = .70
Sell: March 95 Strike
Price of the sold call: $3.50
Intrinsic value of the sold contract: $0
Yield Calculations:

a. Monthly yield if the stock does not move:

$3.50/$21.20 = 16.5 percent

b. Monthly yield if the stock goes to $95 or above:

i. Calculate the gain from price movement

   $95.00 - $93.84 = $1.16 appreciation in the stock

   $1.16 x .70 (delta of the LEAPS) = $.81 appreciation in the LEAPS

ii. Calculate the gain from selling the call option:

   $3.50

iii. Add these two components of gain to get total profit

   $.81 + $3.50 = $4.31 total gain

iv. Calculate the monthly percentage gain:

   $4.31/ $21.20 = 20 percent monthly percentage gain

c. Monthly yield if the stock declines to $90:

i. Calculate the loss from price movement:

   $93.84 - $90.00 = $-3.84

   $-3.84 x .70 (delta) = $-2.69 depreciation in the value of the LEAPS

ii. Calculate the gain from selling the call option:

   $3.50

iii. Add these two components to get the total profit or loss

   $-2.69 + $3.50 = $.81

iv. Calculate the monthly percentage gain:

   $.81/ $21.20 = 3.8 percent

Note 1:

In calculation c above, there is a 3.8 percent yield for the month, even though the stock *declined* $3.84, or 4.1 percent, during the month.

Here, the covered call sold against a LEAPS position has less risk than a stock ownership position. This risk reduction is offset by the forfeiture of the possibility of a large gain through the appreciation in the price of the common stock in a single month.

If an investor achieves yields approximately as calculated in this example on a consistent basis, then the odds are that this forfeiture is of little consequence in the long run.

Note 2:

It is *not* calculated in this analysis that there will be deterioration in the value of the LEAPS during the month. If you originally purchased a LEAPS with a low theta (time decay), and you maintain your LEAPS position until no more than seven months prior to expiration, then this amount should be minimal. I do not recommend that one use long-term options that expire in less than seven months as an underlying position. If you own a LEAPS against which you are selling calls every month, then sell this position and move it out to the LEAPS in the next year at such time that its expiration date is less than this seven-month time point.

Note 3:

If the stock price appreciates to $95 (the short strike), do not let the short option be exercised. A LEAPS will not satisfy a call; it is only a risk hedge. You should buy back this option prior to expiration. You may buy it back for more than the price at which you sold it, but this loss will be more than made up in the appreciation of the LEAPS. The LEAPS should always maintain a higher delta than the sold front month option. If price movement causes this relationship to change, then sell the LEAPS that you hold and purchase another one with a higher delta.

CHAPTER 12

The Secret of Synthetic Stock Positions

> There are plenty of good five-cent cigars in this country. The trouble is they cost a quarter.
> —**Franklin P. Adams**

Through the use of option contracts, one can set up numerous hedge positions and numerous synthetic stock positions. In this book, we will go over two of the most basic synthetic stock ownership positions. If you are someone whose livelihood would be greatly enhanced if his portfolio is profitable, then consideration should be given to using these in determining your overall portfolio position.

The synthetic stock position

You can create a synthetic stock position using options. The method is to simply sell a put ATM and buy a call ATM.

In this example, the deltas of the two positions will add to a sum equal to 1.0, and the appreciation or depreciation will be exactly the same as if you bought the stock.

This method is useful, if you want to do either of the following:

1. Create the equivalent of an ownership position in an index such as the SPX, which does not offer stock. This same position can be established by purchasing shares in the ETF with the symbol SPY. The index position is more desirable to professional traders, however, because of the resulting lower commissions from dealing in a high-priced issue, and because it is cash settled rather than securities settled. There are possible tax advantages to cash settled securities.
2. Establish a stock ownership position for less capital cost than purchasing the stock.

A short stock or index position can also be established with options. Simply do the opposite—sell a call and buy a put. Your result of ownership will be exactly the same as if you had sold the index or stock short.

The synthetic covered call

A covered call position can be established by following the practices I have gone over in this book. Buy the stock, and sell a call against it. The sold call contract should be in the front month and either at the money or slightly out of the money (above the present price of the stock.) If you are very conservative and desire to maintain as low a chance as possible of incurring a loss in exchange for a slightly lower return, then you should sell a call that is slightly in the money and expect to get called out in return for a monthly yield which is usually in the range of 1.5 to 2 percent. This yield is still an 18–24 percent per year return, and outperforms almost all money managers or mutual funds.

This exact same position can be duplicated simply by selling a naked put that is one strike out of the money. In the case of a put, "out of the money" means *below* the current price of the stock. If your broker will allow you to complete this transaction, it usually takes less capital than a covered call. In most market conditions, this position will normally allow you to achieve a monthly yield equal to 2–5 percent per month. You will keep this money if the stock does not come down to the strike price. If the stock *does* come down to the strike price, then the stock will be put to you and you will purchase the stock at a price that was below the market price at the time of the initial transaction. In other words, it is actually a position with less risk than buying stock! This reduced risk is offset by the forfeiture of unlimited upside in the event of a rapid run-up in price. The premise of the strategy set forth in this book, however, is risk reduction and steady monthly income.

If you desire less risk and the accompanying lower yield, then sell a naked put that is two strikes out of the money. The odds of it getting called are less than selling at a higher strike, but the yield is smaller.

If you have the stock put to you, then you own it. Do two things:

1. Set up a stop loss sell point, just as if you had originally bought the stock outright. It is even possible to

do this by creating a contingent short sale below a price resistance level even before the stock is put to you. In other words, you will have sold the stock short prior to your forced purchase of it, and the two positions will negate each other.

2. If you own the stock, be sure to then sell a call in the next month in order to obtain your continuing monthly yield. If you want to minimize your risk, then sell the next month call slightly ITM. If you get called out, it will usually result in a high monthly yield calculated on the low purchase price that resulted from having the stock put to you.

CHAPTER 13

Protect Your Profits through Hedging

> You should invest in companies that even a fool can run, because someday a fool will.
> —Warren Buffet

Buy protective puts correctly

You should always hedge your portfolio against a catastrophe!

On September 11, 2001, there was an attack which destroyed the World Trade Center and killed approximately 3,500 people. This caused the closing of the major financial markets and led to a recession. The stock markets went down, and many people lost some of their savings or retirement accounts.

In 2008, there was a financial crisis that resulted in an approximate decline of 40 percent in the major stock indexes. Many people's portfolios will never recover from this decline, and their retirement will not be the same as they had envisioned as recently as in 2007.

It is quite possible that the United States will have another terrorist attack in the future. It is also possible that this next attack will be biological or even nuclear, and that as many as one million people will be killed. I do not know if this attack will be next month or in twenty years, but I do know that I do not want to be financially wiped out if it happens. I also do not want to be wiped out if an all-out war breaks out in the volatile Middle East. Therefore, I recommend that everyone use protective puts as a hedge against the next catastrophe or unforeseen economic event.

The method of doing this depends on the size and nature of your portfolio. You cannot depend on sell stops to protect you, because the markets will gap down or perhaps even close for an extended period of time when a crisis occurs. In this event, you may not be able to get orders executed.

> **$VIX:** The volatility index of the S&P 500 Index, it is sometimes called the fear factor index, because it rises when the general level of the stock market falls (fear is high), and it declines when the general level of the stock market rises (fear is low). When volatility is high, then option prices are high. This is because the time value, or extrinsic value, portion of option premiums is also high.

I would recommend using far OTM puts as your protection. Weigh the cost of near-month puts versus puts further out in time or even LEAPS puts. This relationship is always changing depending on the current volatility of the market (**$VIX**). In general, if the volatility is high, you will want to buy near-month puts. If the volatility is *very* low, you may want to buy puts that expire in the distant future. Be aware, however, that distant future puts may be more costly in the long run, because if the market moves up, their strike or value point becomes quite far OTM and thus has very little protective value.

If you are using near-month puts, then you should buy new puts each month just prior to, or immediately after, the expiration of your existing puts. If all goes well, all of the puts will expire worthless. You will probably not be able to sell them back, because, as their expiration date approaches, they become worthless (unless they become *very* valuable).

Do not be discouraged by losing money on these puts every month. They are to be regarded as an insurance policy—just as you pay for insurance on your house or your automobile but hope that you don't have to use it.

Insure Your Portfolio with Protective Puts

In order to insure an entire portfolio with a specific contract (though not just one contract), use puts on a broad index, such as the $SPX, $NDX, or the $RUT. In order to determine how much to spend on insurance each month, compare it to your proposed income for the month and do not let it exceed a percentage of your monthly income (say 3–6 percent). You should examine the cost versus the return on a risk graph. If your broker does not provide risk graphs free of charge, then you should consider changing to a different broker.

See Exhibit 15 for a graphic illustration of how the purchase of protective puts can save you from being wiped out in an overnight or one-day gap due to an unforeseen catastrophe, such as a war in the Middle East. Exhibit 15 is a graphic illustration of the price movement of the SPX (S&P 500 Index) on April 3, 2010. On this day, the S&P 500 was at 1178.

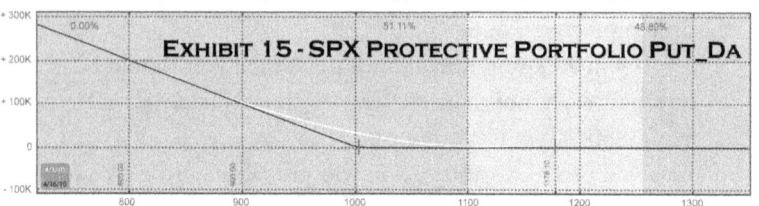

This illustrates the purchase of a total of 10 put contracts with a strike price of 1000, which expire on April 16, being purchased for $.40 each or a total cost equal to $400. These puts give one the right to sell 1000 share equivalents of SPX (10 contracts x 100 shares per contract) for a price of $1,000 each.

Obviously these contracts have very little value on the date of purchase with the current level at 1178. If, at expiration on April 16, the S&P 500 falls below a level of 1000, these contracts will have intrinsic value and will begin to become very valuable. If the S&P 500 reaches a level of 900, the position becomes worth an amount of $102,053. If the S&P 500 reaches a level equal to 800, these puts become worth an amount equal to $199,537.

From this example, you can see that, with a small insurance premium cost of $400 per month, you can protect the value of a large portfolio of stocks or even a portfolio of LEAPS.

It is common for most people to pay this amount of money to insure their home or their automobile. In fact, we do it without even thinking about it. We use insurance for almost every important area of our lives. But, very few people insure their most important asset: their portfolio or retirement account. They leave it almost totally unprotected. This does not make sense!

Do not make this mistake. Be as professional with your money and your retirement account as you are with everything else in your life. Keep protective puts in place.

CONCLUSION

> Apply yourself. Get all the education you can, but then…do something. Don't just stand there, make it happen!
> —**Lee Iacocca**

In conclusion, this book was written for several groups of people that desire financial independence and security. They are summarized as follows:

1. The individual who has found himself in a position of needing more income to live upon than his retirement plan can provide at the low traditional rates of return provided by most money managers. You need to manage your own money!

2. The young person who desires to start an investment savings program now and make it grow steadily over

the years so he can retire early and have the life that most people only dream about.

3. The individual who has an income and a retirement plan and desires not only more income, but also more time with his family.

This book is not for the casual reader. It is for the serious individual that is ready to study the strategies explained herein until he has a full understanding of how to use them. Once you begin this journey to financial security through high return, low risk investing, you're on a never-ending mission to have an exciting and fulfilling life. Life is definitely more fun if you have the means by which to do the things that you want to do and go where you want to go.

Take the time to follow up:

- Study this book over several times until you understand and feel comfortable in implementing your own income strategies.
- Go to www.incomestrategiesacademy.com and begin to think about keeping up with your investing on a daily basis.
- Most importantly, seriously consider attending a live seminar, where you can communicate with other people who make their living using the strategies taught in this book, as well as other, more advanced strategies. As you become more and more successful, you will want to learn these advanced strategies also.

If you stop here and do not do any follow up or continuing education, then you will have wasted your time and sacrificed the fulfillment that you and your family could have enjoyed with financial independence.

You have completed this book, but your learning has just begun!

I wish you the best of luck in your studies, and success in your investing strategies. I hope to see you at one of the seminars, because if I do, this means that you are well on the way to fulfilling your financial goals and making your dreams come true.

APPENDIX 1

A Look at Directional Trading

I do not suggest that there is only one right way to trade the stock market. There are many methods and strategies that can be used to make or lose money in the stock market. However, I believe that only smart, focused, and rule-based active trading can consistently generate investment returns that exceed those derived from a buy-and-hold strategy—or as I like to call it, "Buying, hoping, and praying."

A "buy, hope, and pray" trader buys a stock and then hopes and prays that it will move higher. The truth is that everyone who buys a long equity position hopes its share price will move higher. But far too many stock traders make the mistake of relying more on a hope and prayer than on smart trading.

When I put on a trade, I always assume that the trade might go wrong. In other words, that I have picked the wrong stock at the wrong time and that its share price will move significantly against me. Therefore, I always have an exit plan for every trade. Of course, I "hope" for the best, but I always "plan for the worst." Even the best stock market investor in the world has losing trades in the normal course of action. The key is to have the losing trades cost you far less than the winning trades show in profits.

So, when do you make the decision to get out of a losing trade? That is the question! "Buy and hold," or following the buy, hope, and pray philosophy, dictates that if you hold onto a stock long enough, it will eventually recover and generate a profit. But acting in accordance with this school of thought can lead you into a situation wherein your holdings continue to move lower or languish in a losing position for months or even years! So how do you make a decision about when to change course and go to the next investment?

This is the dilemma in which every investor finds himself all too often. They know *what* they want to buy, they know *when* they want to buy, and they may even know *at what price* they want to buy. Some investors may even know their target, or the price at which they want to sell if the stock moves higher. However, the vast majority of stock market investors do not know when they should sell a losing position. They really have difficulty selling what they believe to be a fundamentally strong stock when, in their mind, the stock just should not be trading lower. Often, they try to convince themselves that the market is wrong. They believe that if they just hold on a little longer, their stock will recover. This is *not* smart trading; this is emotional trading! It is "hope and pray" trading. This kind of trading can result in a person losing a substantial portion of their funds.

The key to making consistent profits in the stock market is to know not only what to buy and when to buy, but also when to sell. "When to sell" means the price at which to set a definite stop loss as well as the price which is the target.

I offer a fairly simple "Stop Loss Strategy." To start, of course, I only want to buy or be long in equities that are trending higher. If I am shorting, I only want to be short in equities that are trending lower. I will then hold that position as long as the stock price does not reverse its trend. When a trend reversal occurs, I will get out of the trade. An uptrend reversal is detected by a lower high and a lower low (the beginning of a downtrend). A downtrend reversal is detected by a higher high and a higher low (the beginning of an uptrend).

All equities fluctuate in price on a minute-by-minute, day-by-day, week-by-week, month-by-month, and year-by-year basis. The real key is to know the difference between normal volatility and a change in the trend. If an equity position is fluctuating due to normal volatility, then I want to maintain the position; but, if it changes its overall trend, and actually starts to move against me, then I want to be out as soon as possible.

So, how does one know the difference between normal volatility and a change in trend? After all, a downward movement in normal volatility looks an awful lot like the first downward move in a change in trend. Below is a description of a method that I often use.

First, I calculate the standard deviation of equity's price movement over a five-day period of time (weekly). This volatility is calculated based on the past twelve months' price fluctuation. Now I know how much the price of a stock is expected to move (either up or down) over the next week 68 percent of the time. Next, I subtract that value (for long positions) from the equity's previous week's lowest low. That price then becomes the equity's stop loss. I do the reverse for short positions. These calculations are available on most charting services and should take only a moment of your time. You do not have to be a mathematician in order to use this method of setting stop loss points.

If the equity moves against me enough to trigger this stop in the upcoming week, I exit the trade. Each week, I recalculate the standard deviation and the previous week's low, and I set a new stop loss. I let winners run and eliminate losers by never lowering stops for long positions and never raising them for short positions.

The theory is that this stop loss will remain just below the equity's normal weekly volatility, which gives the equity room to move. But, if the equity's share price touches the stop loss, the assumption is that the equity has moved from normal volatility to a possible change in trend. Of course, this rule is not always correct (nothing in the stock market is), but it is one method of keeping yourself out of trouble or suffering a major setback.

Each experienced trader can set his own additional rules for early detection of a trend change and setting stop losses and targets. I also use a break of the horizontal or vertical trend line, a change in the slope of the weekly MACD histogram, and a penetration of stochastic ranges or of the Bollinger Bands. I use these other rules only to tighten the stop (move it closer to the market price), never to loosen the stop.

Remember that it is not buying at the right time that makes you money; it is selling at the right time.

APPENDIX 2

How to "Shoot for the Stars" without Losing Your Shirt

Have you ever wanted to take a large position in a stock or a commodity about which you felt positive, but were afraid to do so because its high volatility might cause you to incur a loss that is too large for your portfolio? The same might be true for a "hot" stock that you want to own, but feared that the recent run-up in price might reverse itself and leave you "holding the bag."

You can consider limiting your risk while still being able to take advantage of these situations by learning how to use protective put options as a means of stopping your losses. Let's look at an example:

Let's say that on April 12, 2010, we believe that gold will go higher over the coming year. We have seen gold run up by a considerable amount during the last year, and we know that its price is very volatile. Therefore, we are afraid to buy a position that is meaningful, because a decline of, say, 10 percent would set our portfolio back quite a bit. What is a reasonable investment for us to consider?

We know that there is an ETF that owns gold bullion; its symbol is GLD. On today's date, GLD closed at $113.10 per share. If we look at a May options table for GLD (the April options are too close to expiration), we see that we can buy a May 109 put option on GLD for $1.08 per share. Thus we can limit our losses on the ownership position to $113.10-$109.00 = $4.10 per share plus the cost of the option of $1.08 per share. This total exposure is therefore equal to $4.10 + $1.08 = $5.18 per share or 4.6 percent maximum loss on the position. Therefore, a 100 share position with a value of $11,310 would have a maximum loss of $518. If, on the other hand, the ETF rises in value by, say, 15 percent to $130, your position would be worth $13,000 for a $1,582.00 profit.

The appreciation possibility is unlimited. Notice that the cost of insurance protection is $1.08 per month or less than 1 percent per month of the price of the position. Do not take this type of hedge unless you believe that the underlying security will appreciate much more than the 1 percent per month or 12 percent per year that the put options will cost you.

Exhibit 16 provides a graphic illustration of this example. You can see that the flat price line beginning at 109 and going all the way to zero indicates that the put has limited your loss to a maximum amount. As the price of GLD rises, the profits are unlimited.

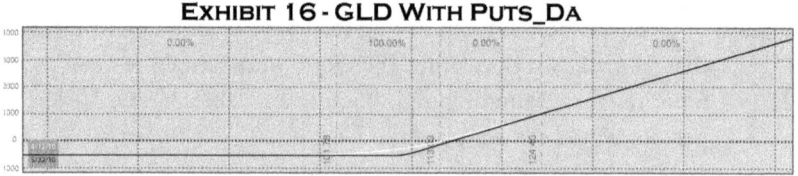

Exhibit 16 - GLD With Puts_DA

As you approach the expiration date of the put options, you should sell these May put options and buy June put options. If the price of GLD has risen during the month, you will probably want to buy options with a higher strike price than 109. These new put options with a higher strike will lock in your profits over time as the price of the underlying security rises.

APPENDIX 3
Glossary

American Style Option: An option contract that can be exercised at any time up to the time of expiration. The other type of option is the European Style Option, which can be exercised only at expiration. Most stock options are American Style, and most Index options are European Style.

Arbitrage: The simultaneous purchase or sale of two securities whose risk factors offset each other while providing or locking-in a profit spread between the two positions. As an example, it is sometimes possible to buy oil contracts at today's price, take delivery, and at the same time sell them at a higher price in the futures market six to nine months out. This tactic will result in a profit if the price differential between the purchase price and the sell price is greater than the storage cost plus the interest-carrying charges on the funds that are tied up. In this example, there is no risk of price movement either up or down, because the long and short positions are taken at the same point in time and offset each other.

Ask Price: The lowest price that a seller on an exchange will accept for securities or other assets at a given moment in time.

At-The-Money (ATM): If an option has a strike price approximately equal to the price of its underlying security, then it is said to be At-The-Money.

Automatic Exercise: If an option expires with intrinsic value relative to its underlying security, then it is accepted practice for the brokerage firm to automatically exercise it. If you do not want this to happen to you (there is normally a commission and a capital requirement), then you should sell and realize your profit prior to expiration.

Bare Cash: A company's cash plus liquid assets, less its debts that must be repaid within one year. In the 1930s, Professors Graham and Dodd recommended buying companies when they could be purchased for their bare cash value.

Bear: An investor that believes that a stock or the market is expected to fall.

Bear Market: A stock market cycle in which prices of the broad indexes fall at least 20 percent over a period lasting at least two quarters. It is usually accompanied by a weak economy and declining corporate profits.

Bid Price: The offered price by market makers or an exchange to buy a stock, index, or option.

Black-Scholes Formula: A Nobel-Prize-winning pricing model that is used by options exchanges to price options. It considers such factors as the price of the underlying security, option strike price, time remaining until expiration, implied volatility, and the current level of interest rates.

Break-even: The price (usually at the expiration of an option) at which the transaction neither makes nor loses money.

Bull: An investor that believes that a stock or the general level of the stock market is expected to rise.

Bull Market: A stock market cycle in which prices of the broad indexes rise for an extended period of time. It is usually during a time of an expanding economy and increasing corporate profits.

Buy Limit: The maximum amount that the customer will allow his broker to pay to purchase an asset.

Call Option: A contract that gives the holder the right, but not the obligation, to buy a specific stock at a specific strike price on or before a certain date in time.

Chicago Board Options Exchange (CBOE): The largest options exchange in the United States.

Commission: A fee that is charged by the brokerage firm that handles a transaction.

Compound or Compound Interest: The effect that arises when earned interest is added to principal, so that from that moment on, the interest that has been added *itself* earns interest. This addition of interest to the principal is called *compounding* (in other words, the interest is compounded).

Contingency Order: An order that is placed with a broker but cannot be executed until a certain event occurs. This event is usually based upon the future price movement of the security. In most circumstances, contingency orders allow the investor to rely on the fact that his stop loss will not be greatly exceeded except in the event of a large price gap.

Covered Call: A short position in a call contract that is offset or hedged by a long position in the underlying stock or other asset.

Covered Put: A short position in a put contract that is offset or hedged by a short position in the underlying stock or other asset.

Directional Trading: A position or combination of positions in securities and/or options that rely upon appreciation or depreciation in the price of such security in order for the trade to be profitable.

Delta: The change in the price of an option that will occur with a one-point change in the price of the underlying instrument. If a call has a delta of .50, then its price will move up or down by $.50 when the price of the underlying stock moves up or down by $1.00.

ETF: Exchange Traded Fund. An investment fund that is traded on stock exchanges, much like stocks. An ETF holds assets, such as stocks or bonds, and trades at approximately the same price as the net asset value of its underlying assets over the course of the trading day. Most ETFs track either an index, such as the S&P 500, or stocks in a specific industry or sector. For this reason, the specific stocks do not change often as with an actively managed mutual fund. ETFs may be attractive as investments because of their low management fees, tax efficiency, and stock-like features.

European Style Option: A call or put option that can be exercised only at the time of its expiration.

Exponential Moving Average (EMA): An average of past prices that is weighted to give greater influence to the most recent data. It therefore responds faster to changing input.

Exercise: Putting into effect an option holder's rights to buy or sell an underlying security at a specific strike price.

Expiration: The date and time after which an option can no longer be exercised.

Extrinsic Value: That portion of the price of an option that cannot be attributed to its strike price versus the price of the underlying security. This is also sometimes referred to as "time value" or "juice."

Fundamental Analysis: The process of accessing the value of a company's stock by studying its historical financial and accounting records and its forecasts for the future. This valuation assessment is then compared to the current market price of the stock in order to form a buy or sell opinion or recommendation.

Gamma: Options Gamma is the change in the price of an option that will occur with a one-point move in the option's delta.

Good Till Canceled Order (GTC): An order that remains in effect until it is cancelled. This is compared to a normal order that is good for the day only. A GTC order is usually used to place a buy or sell stop on an existing position.

Implied Volatility: The expected future (as opposed to historical) rate of change in the price of a financial asset; implied volatility is a major factor in determining the price of options.

Index: A compilation of stocks that are averaged together in order to obtain a price reading or measurement. Broad-based indexes such as the S&P 500 (SPX), Dow Jones Industrials (DJI), Russell 2000 (RUT), and the NASDAQ 100 (NDX) are the most commonly used indexes. There are also many narrow-based indexes. The use of these instruments allows the holder to invest based on broad economic factors as opposed to company-specific events.

Index Options: Call and put options in an underlying index.

In The Money (ITM): If a call option has a strike price that is lower than the current market price of the underlying security, this means that if its price remains unchanged, the call option will have value at expiration and is said to be "in the money." At expiration, the "in the money" value is the only value remaining. Likewise, a put option has value at expiration if its strike price is above the price of the underlying security.

Intrinsic Value: A call option has intrinsic value if its strike price is lower than the price of the underlying security. The difference between these two prices is the intrinsic value. Intrinsic value plus extrinsic value is equal to the price of an option. There is no remaining extrinsic value at expiration; therefore, at this point in time, intrinsic value will always be equal to the price of the option.

LEAPS: This term refers to Long-term Equity Appreciation Participation Securities. These are options with expiration dates at least six months, and not longer than three years, in the future.

Leverage: In finance, leverage refers to the use of debt to supplement an investment. This use will generally substantially increase or decrease the percentage return on investment.

Limit Order: An order that is placed with a maximum price to be paid in the case of a buy, or long position, or a minimum price with respect to a sell, or short position.

Long Position: If a stock or other position is owned, one is said to be long in it.

Margin: A loan from a brokerage firm to its account holder that is made in order to acquire a larger position than permitted by the available cash in the account. Regulation T of the Securities and Exchange Commission determines the amount or loan to value ratio that can be extended. This ratio changes from time to time.

Margin Requirement: The amount of cash that is required to be in an account in order to execute or maintain a particular transaction.

Market Order: An order that is placed with directions to the brokerage firm to execute at the prevailing price at that moment in time. Unfortunately, orders placed at market are often taken advantage of by brokerage firms, specialists, or market makers.

Naked Call: A sold, or short, call position that is not supported by any underlying security or hedge position. The maximum risk of a naked call is unlimited. Many brokerages do not permit naked short options except for the most experienced and well capitalized investors.

Naked Put: A sold or short put position that is not supported by any underlying security or hedge position. The maximum risk is the strike price, if the stock goes to zero.

Naked Transaction: A sell of any right of ownership which the seller or writer does not either own outright or have backed up by a hedge position. Thus, his position is not covered and his losses can be unlimited.

NASDAQ: The National Association of Securities Dealers Automated Quotations is a computerized system that allows brokers and dealers to get quotes and to trade the stocks that qualify to be listed.

New York Stock Exchange (NYSE): The largest stock market exchange in the world. Only stocks in listed companies are traded here.

Non-directional Trade: A position or combination of positions in stocks and/or options that is designed to be profitable if the underlying security trades within a narrow range rather than appreciating or depreciating by a large amount.

Option: A security that gives the holder the right to buy (call option) or to sell (put option) a particular asset at a certain price (the strike price) on or before a certain date (the expiration date). This is a right to exercise; it is not an obligation to do so.

Option Greeks: The five mathematical calculations that determine the price of an option. These are as follows: delta, theta, gamma, rho, and vega.

Option Holder: The owner of a call or a put option.

Option Premium: The price that a holder pays in order to acquire or to sell an option.

Option Spread: A simultaneous purchase and sell of two different options in hope that the difference between their prices (the spread) will accrue to the benefit of the investor as either the price of the underlying security changes or the time value of the two options evaporates.

Option Writer: An investor that sells an option is referred to as its writer. This option writer has the obligation to either buy or sell at the strike price at expiration or when exercised.

Out of The Money (OTM): A call option is OTM when its strike price is above the price of the underlying security. A put option is OTM when its strike price is below the price of the underlying security. If an option is OTM at expiration, then it has no value.

Premium: In reference to an option, the amount per contract that an option buyer pays to the seller.

Put Option: A contract that gives the holder the right, but not the obligation, to sell a security at a specific price (strike) either on or before a certain date (expiration).

Regression to the Mean: A statistical term which refers to the fact that things usually return to normal or the way that they were before. In reference to financial pricing, this means that prices do not generally move more than one standard deviation, based upon historical volatility, before they reverse course and head back to their prior average.

Resistance: A price level at which a security hits selling pressure and thus usually begins to fall in price.

Return on Investment: The profit or loss resulting from a financial transaction divided by the cost of such a transaction. This is usually calculated or expressed as a percentage at an annual rate.

Rho: The change in the price of an option contract that results from a 1 percent change in interest rates.

Security: A trading instrument that evidences an ownership interest. Such interest can be either in common or preferred stock, bonds, options, or other investments.

Short Position: A position in a security wherein it has been sold, but it has not yet been bought. In order to close out this transaction, this security must be purchased. One would desire to be short if he believed that the value of the security will decline.

Slippage: The amount of money that is lost on each trade that is attributable to the fact that one must buy at or near the asked price and sell at or near the offered price.

Spread: The difference between the bid and ask prices of a security. Also, this term may refer to the difference or intended profit between the prices of two arbitraged securities.

Stock: Evidence of an ownership position in a company.

Stop Loss Order: An order that directs the brokerage firm to automatically exit a position based upon the occurrence of a certain event. This event is usually related to the achievement of a price level of the security or, in the case of a derivative, the price level of the underlying security. This is a sell order in the case of a long position and a buy order in the case of a short position.

Stop Loss: A price or other point, such as a certain dollar amount of loss at which a position will be exited and the losses will therefore be stopped.

Straddle: An option position wherein one either buys or sells both a naked call and a naked put on the same security, at the same strike price, and for the same expiration date.

Strangle: An option position wherein one either buys or sells both a naked call and a naked put on the same security for the same expiration date. However, the two positions have different strike prices.

Strike Price: The price at which a call or put option can be exercised.

Support: A price level at which a security finds buying power and thus usually begins to rise in price.

Target: Either the price or a specific dollar profit level at which a position will be exited. It is generally the goal or desired outcome of a trade.

Technical Analysis: A method of evaluating and forecasting the future price of a security by observing and measuring certain mathematical relationships between past price movement, volume, and volatility.

Theta: Theta is a measurement of the daily rate of depreciation of an option contract's price based upon the assumption that the underlying stock remains stagnant. Thus, it is referring to the loss in value that is due to the passing of time or extrinsic value depreciation.

Time Value: Also known as extrinsic value, it is that portion of the price of an option that cannot be attributed to its strike price versus the price of the underlying security. This is also sometimes referred to as "juice."

Triple Witching Day: The third Friday in March, June, September, and December (end of the quarter). This is when U.S. stock options, futures options, and index options all expire on the same day.

Uncovered Call: Also referred to as a naked call, this is a sold call position that is not hedged or supported by a long position in the underlying security.

Uncovered Put: Also referred to as a naked put, this is a sold put position that is not also hedged or supported by a short position in the underlying security.

Vega: The change in the price of an option that is due to a change in the implied volatility of the underlying security.

$VIX: The volatility index of the S&P 500 Index, it is sometimes called the fear factor index, because it rises when the general level of the stock market falls (fear is high), and it declines when the general level of the stock market rises (fear is low). When volatility is high, then option prices are high. This is because the time value, or extrinsic value, portion of option premiums is also high.

Writer: A seller of an option that has an *obligation* to perform.

APPENDIX 4

Exhibits

Exhibit 1 - POT Trendline

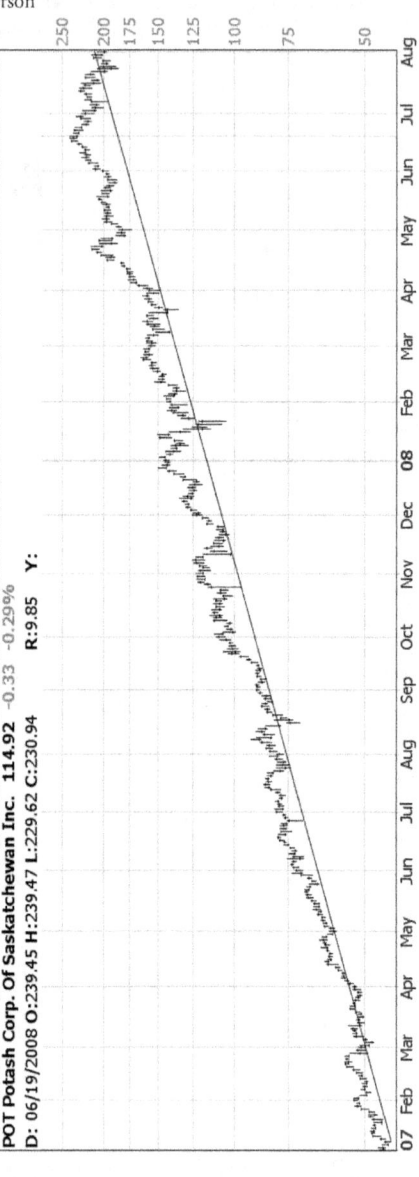

Hard Times Easy Trading | 163

Exhibit 2 - C Trendline

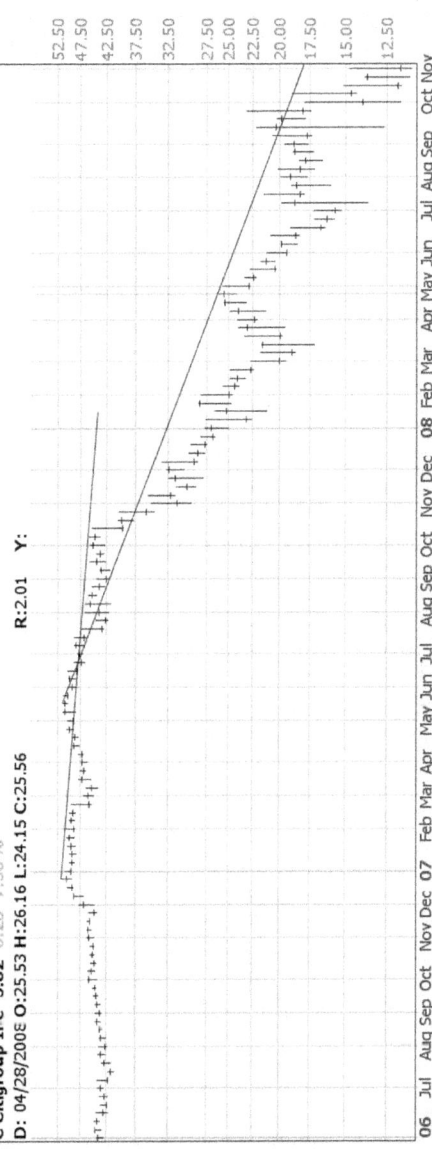

164 | Jim Peterson

Exhibit 3 - MCD Trendline & Channel

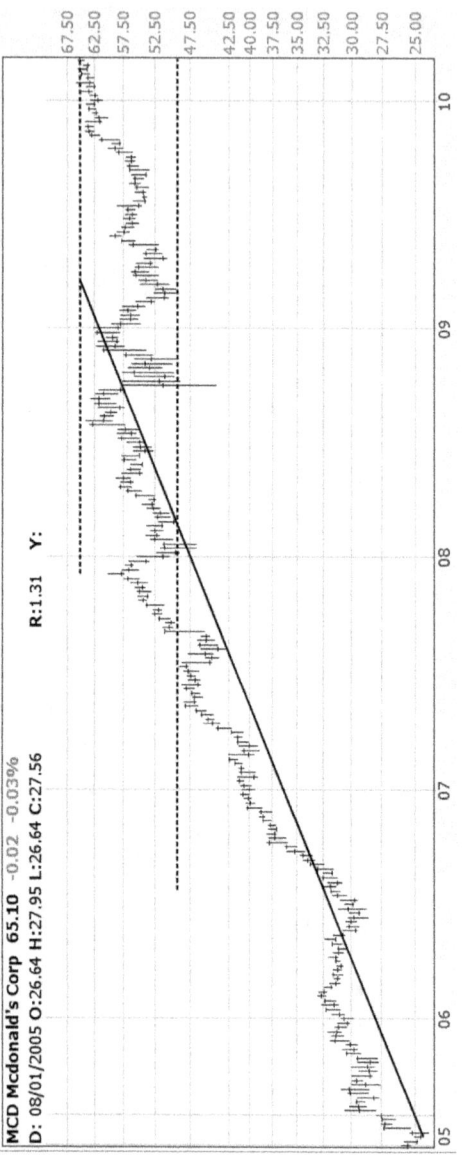

Exhibit 4 - SPX - Moving averages

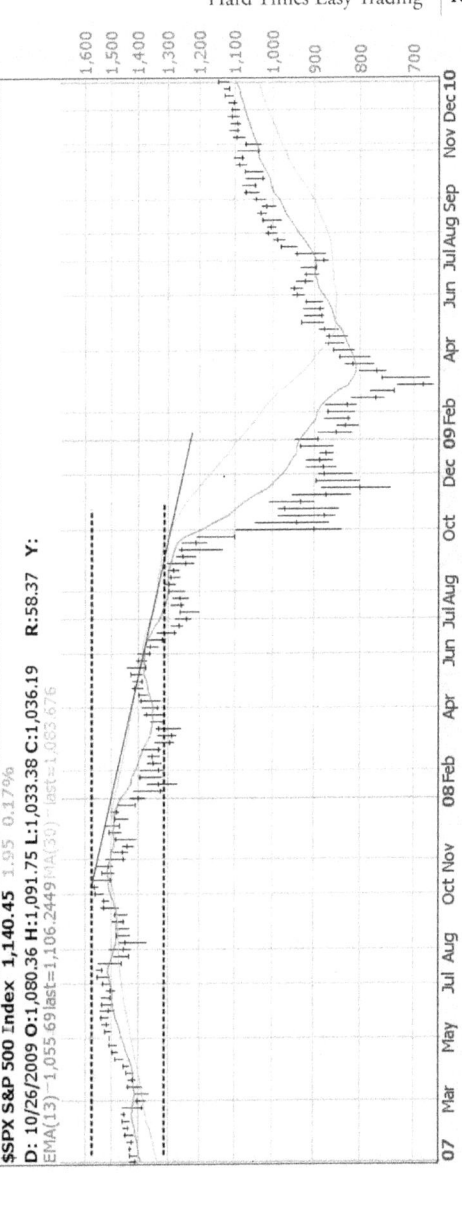

Exhibit 5 - RUT - Daily MACD

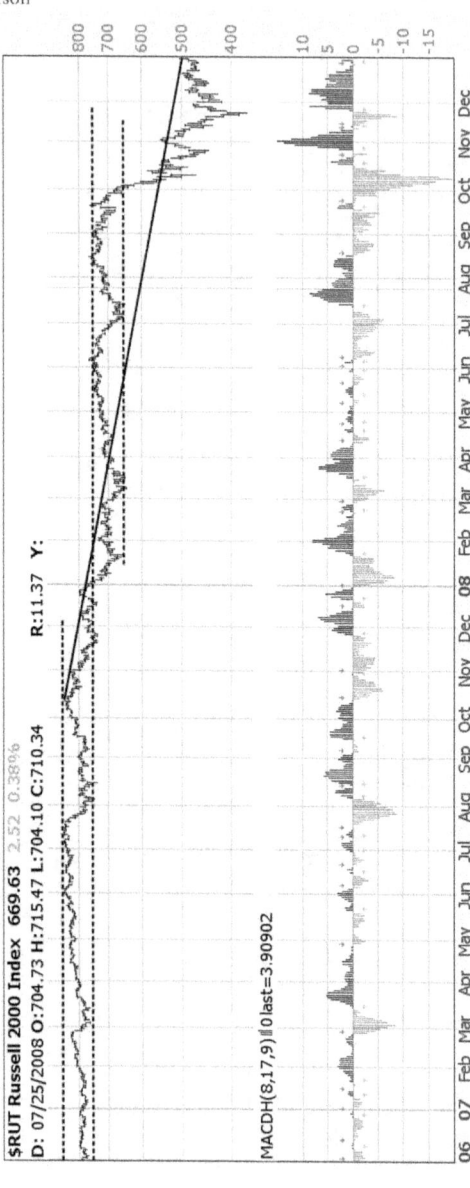

Hard Times Easy Trading | 167

Exhibit 6 - RUT Weekly MACD

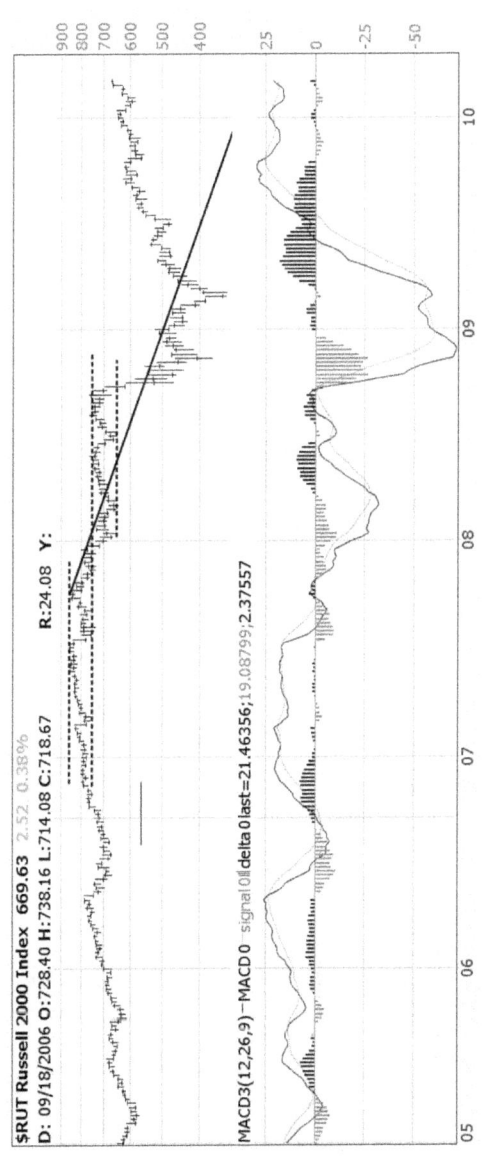

168 | Jim Peterson

Exhibit 7 - Daily chart Stochastics

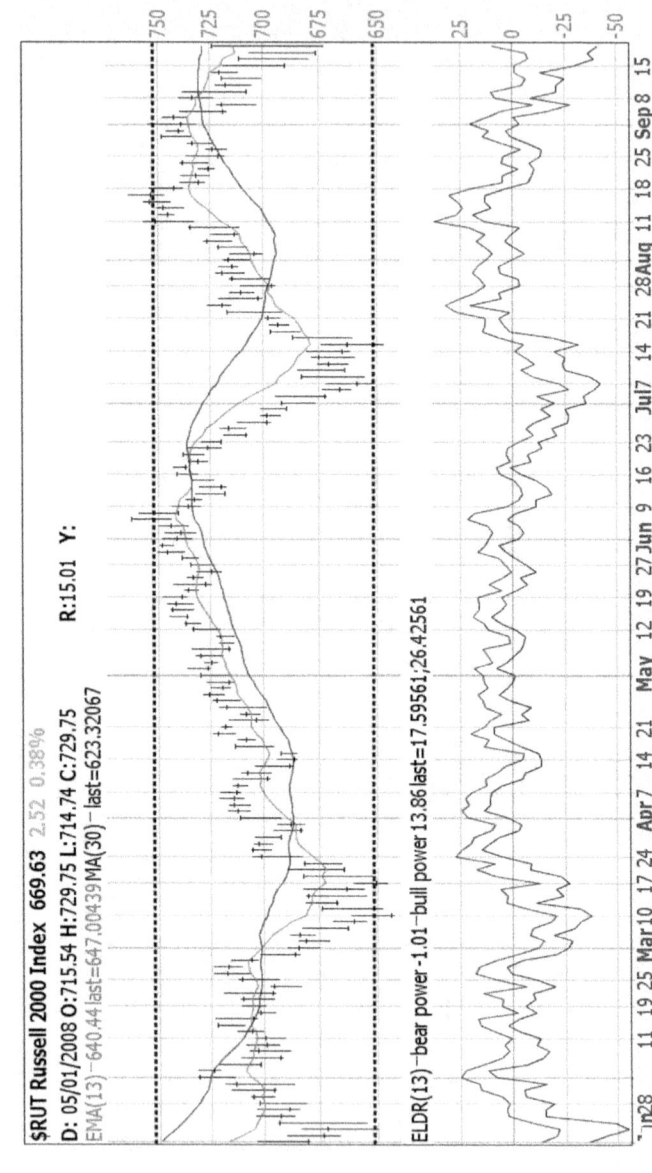

Exhibit 8 - RUT - Moving Averages & Elder

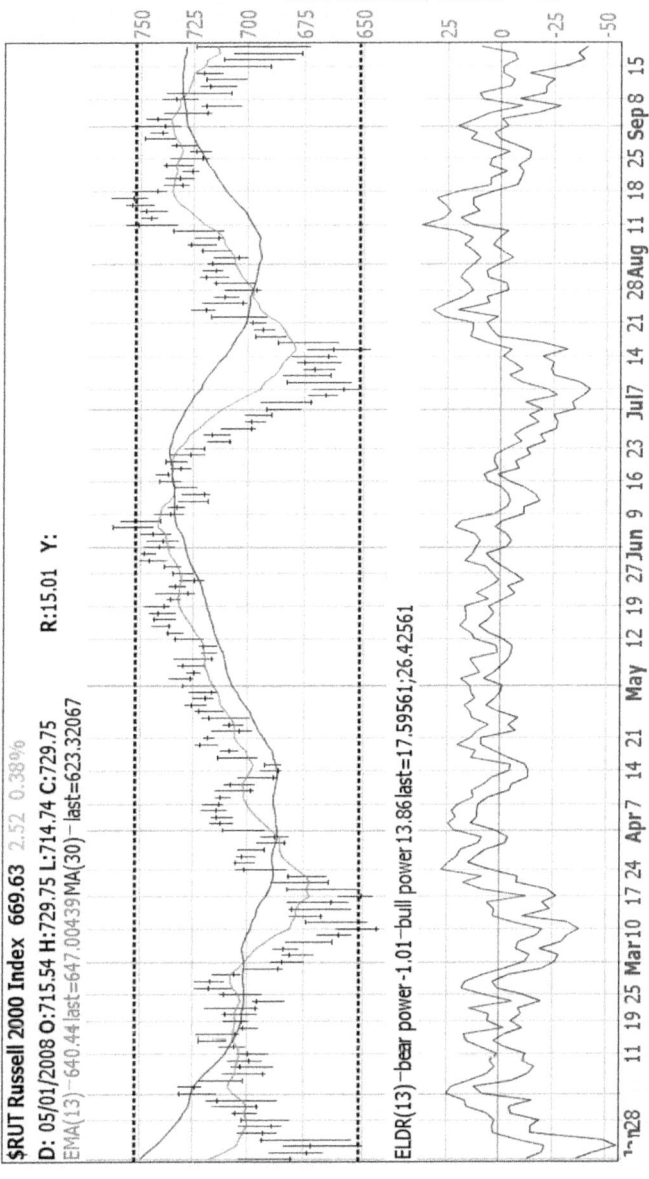

Exhibit 9 - New - IBM - Bollinger Bands

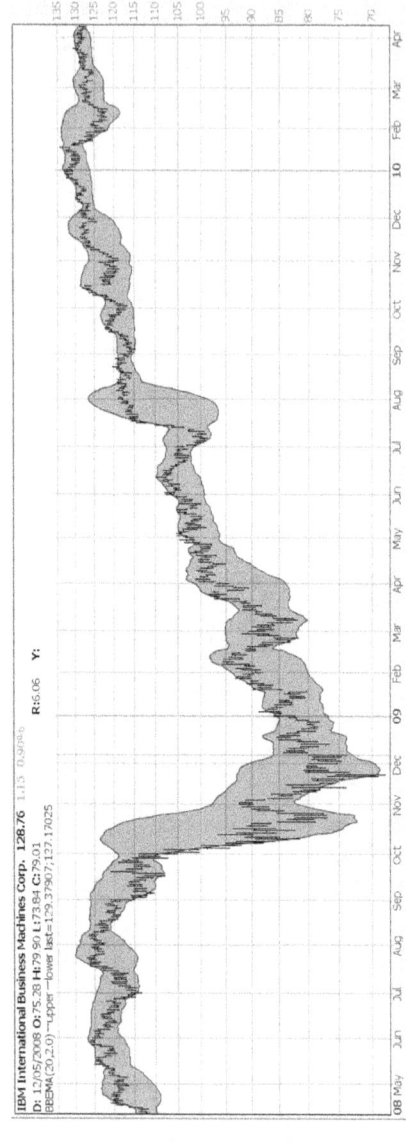

Hard Times Easy Trading | 171

Exhibit 10 - Weekly POT

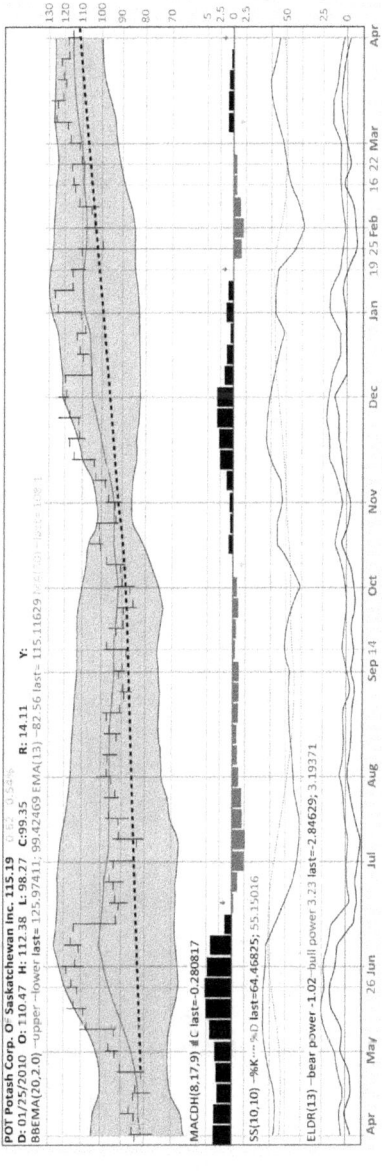

Exhibit 11 - POT Daily Charts - All Indicators

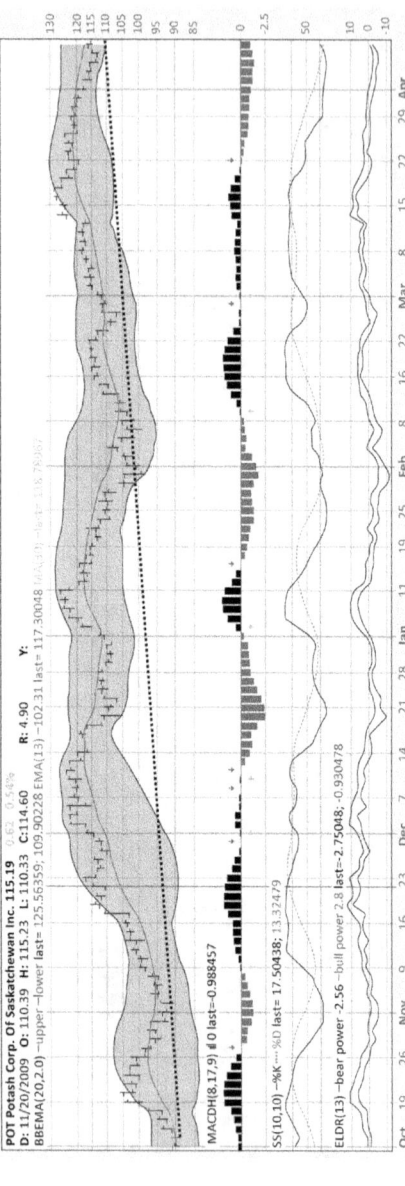

Exhibit 12

9-Apr-10

Options Table

POT Price: $115.19   May 2010 - Expiration   40 Days to expiration

Calls		Strike Price	Puts	
Bid	**Ask**		**Bid**	**Ask**
16	**16.2**	100	1	1.05
12	**12.15**	105	1.97	2.02
8.55	**8.7**	110	3.5	3.6
5.85	6	115	5.8	5.9
3.85	3.95	120	**8.75**	**8.9**
2.44	2.53	125	**12.35**	**12.5**
1.52	1.58	130	**16.4**	**16.55**
0.93	0.98	135	**20.8**	**20.95**

Prices in bold face type are In The Money and therefore have intrinsic value.

Prices in regular type have only time value as of this date.

Exhibit 13

13-Feb-09

Options Table

IBM Price: $93.84   93.84

January 2010 - Expiration   336 Days to expiration

Calls					Strike Price	Puts			
Delta	Open Interest	Intrinsic	Bid	Ask		Bid	Ask	Delta	Open Interest	Intrinsic
0.87	79	38.84	40.2	41.3	55	2.3	2.45	0.09	1279	0
0.85	286	33.84	36	37	60	3	3.3	0.12	3956	0
0.82	41	28.84	31.9	32.6	65	4	4.3	0.15	3531	0
0.79	862	23.84	28.1	28.5	70	5.2	5.4	0.19	4256	0
0.75	77	18.84	24.4	24.7	75	6.4	6.8	0.23	3135	0
0.7	1621	13.84	21	21.4	80	7.9	8.4	0.28	5914	0
0.65	1090	8.84	17.9	18.2	85	9.7	10.2	0.34	2595	0
0.6	7002	3.84	15	15.3	90	11.8	12.3	0.39	6158	0
0.54	**1871**	**0**	**12.5**	**12.7**	**95**	**14.1**	**14.7**	**0.45**	**984**	**1.16**
0.48	**9131**	**0**	**10.1**	**10.4**	**100**	**16.7**	**17.3**	**0.52**	**5959**	**6.16**
0.42	**894**	**0**	**8.1**	**8.7**	**105**	**19.6**	**20.4**	**0.58**	**155**	**11.16**

Prices in bold face type are In The Money and therefore have intrinsic value.

Prices in regular type have only time value as of this date.

Exhibit 14

13-Feb-09

Options Table

IBM   Price: $93.84

March 2009 - Expiration   35 Days to expiration

Calls					Strike Price	Puts			
Delta	Open Interest	Intrinsic	Bid	Ask		Bid	Ask	Delta	Open Interest	Intrinsic
0.99	0	38.84	38.6	39.3	55	0	0.1	0.01	279	0
0.97	0	33.84	33.7	34.4	60	0.05	0.15	0.01	455	0
0.95	1	28.84	28.7	29.4	65	0.1	0.2	0.02	858	0
0.93	3	23.84	23.8	24.2	70	0.2	0.3	0.04	1497	0
0.91	108	18.84	19.1	19.4	75	0.4	0.5	0.07	2198	0
0.87	1997	13.84	14.5	14.7	80	0.8	0.85	0.12	5642	0
0.79	1889	8.84	10.2	10.4	85	1.5	1.6	0.21	3298	0
0.65	6550	3.84	6.4	6.6	90	2.7	2.8	0.35	6498	0
0.47	7716	0	3.5	3.6	95	4.7	4.9	0.54	4337	1.16
0.28	10497	0	1.5	1.6	100	7.7	7.9	0.75	2087	6.16
0.13	3868	0	0.5	0.6	105	11.6	11.8	0.95	88	11.16

Prices in bold face type are In The Money and therefore have intrinsic value.
Prices in regular type have only time value as of this date.

Exhibit 15 - SPX Protective Portfolio Put

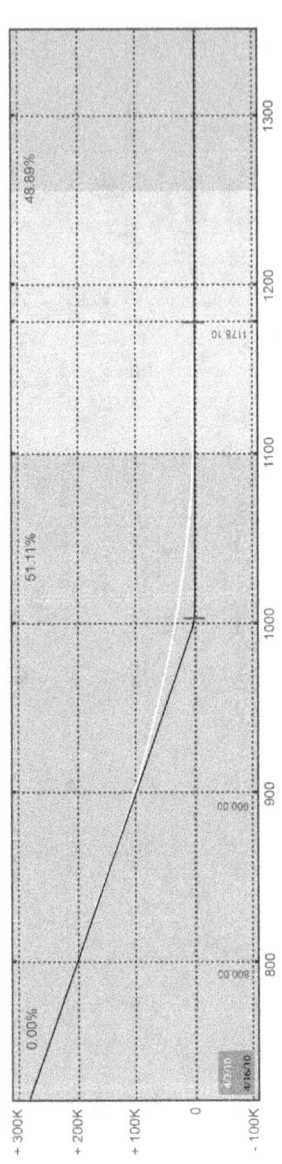

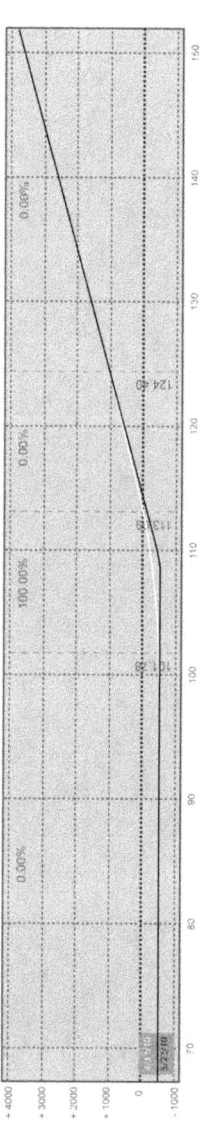

Exhibit 16 - GLD with puts

www.ingramcontent.com/pod-product-compliance
Lightning Source LLC
Chambersburg PA
CBHW070943230426
43666CB00011B/2545